travel

Thames & Hudson

FAMILY**LIFE**STYLE

travel

anita kaushal

with 360 colour illustrations

contents

Taking in the ancient cobbled streets of Cáceres, in Extremadura, Spain, guidebook in hand. Previous pages: The rugged beauty of the Namibian landscape forms the backdrop to Mowani Mountain Camp, near Twyfelfontein, the country's first UNESCO-designated World Heritage Site. Frontispiece: A would-be princess thinks she could get used to a life of tiaras at Dromoland Castle, in Ireland's Co. Clare.

start

travel

Family holidays are a potent mix of intense periods of time spent together, exhilarating moments of discovery, and even (inevitably) the odd calamity or two. They are often the most vivid of our memories as we grow older, with stories that we tell and retell, sometimes with rueful remembrance. The most glamorous getaways are not necessarily the ones that we remember most fondly, although they have their place, and many of the vacation suggestions featured in this book are luxurious, indeed. But the smaller, more mundane holidays have their place in our hearts, too: long hours spent in the car on the way to grandparents have a way of knitting together the family unit, allowing enforced hours of communication and togetherness, and will prompt just as many stories down the road. Whether your holiday is luxurious or more humble, it is this togetherness that counts.

Whatever kind of holiday you choose – a bucket-and-spade weekend at the beach, a once-in-a-lifetime safari adventure, or a short city break – this is unique family time when children can be (reasonably) free of rules and parents can escape the responsibilities of everyday life. While some thought does need to be given to the logistics of travelling to and arriving at our destination, what matters most is that we leave behind our daily routines and experience something new once we get there. Travel broadens our children's thinking, awareness, curiosity and respect for others, and time away can revive our own senses and rejuvenate our souls. It may seem that, since having children, holidays that offer style and indulgence are off the menu, but this need not be the case. In this book you will find exciting and inspirational ideas for vacations that will appeal to all, in the hope that you will return home richer for the experience.

Like its predecessor, the book is divided into four themes, each of which offers practical information supplemented by beautiful photographs of places that you, just like the families shown, may want to include in your holiday plans. First is 'Plan', which looks at the practicalities and necessities of embarking on your journey, as well as discussing the memories and treasures we might bring home with us. 'City' takes a look at the grand architecture and big sights of the great cities, along with the individual urban villages that make them the characterful destinations they are. 'Adventure' is just that, covering all manner of holidays for the free-spirited traveller, from camping to surfing, scaling sand dunes to trekking through the mountains. 'Escape' is all about treating yourself to a new level of indulgence, and children to holidays that will engage their imaginations. Finally, 'Go' offers addresses and websites to help you plan your holiday.

Producing a guidebook that covers the whole of the world would be too big a task. Instead, *FamilyLifeStyle: Travel* gives a flavour of the many types of holidays that are available and will appeal to families. We now seem to have an endless supply of hotel and travel guides, websites, and countless other sources of information, and by focusing so much on what's hot and what's not, we may have lost sight of the deeper meaning of travel. Everyone has their own idea of what holidays mean to them, but we all hope to return refreshed and ready to face our lives again. Children are only young for such a short time, so it is all the more important to take a little time out and fill their hearts and yours with lasting memories.

A priceless education...

While no one would disagree that formal EDUCATION does much to give our children sound *knowledge* and teach them the **value** of discipline, rules and social interaction, it is equally true that it can also leave them occasionally feeling a little over-pressured and jaded. Travel offers a more natural – and equally valuable – way of learning, engaging children's *senses* and INSTINCTS in a way that suits their understanding and personalities. Changing currency, communicating in a different language, experiencing new cultures and customs and *exploring* the world outside – these are the things that BROADEN a child's view of the world and *SPARK* their *curiosity* beyond any classroom environment. The best part is that it all happens while they are having fun.

plan

No routines, no homework, a break from being told what to do and how to live in almost every waking moment – holidays give children a much-needed respite from rules and the chance to run free, make new friends, and see their parents in a new light. Instead of negotiating the minefield of daily obligations, this is a time for both parents and their offspring to get to know each other as individuals. But although vacations are indeed a time of relaxation and enjoyment, they will be even better – as drab as it sounds – with a little careful organization. Not only does planning ahead alleviate the stress caused by last-minute panics, but the act of preparation and packing also serves to heighten children's anticipation and excitement about the adventure that lies before them. The plans we make even before setting off on our holidays are all part of the journey, and spending a bit of time in thought and making lists gives us the opportunity to consider what everyone in the family wants from their precious time away.

Helping children locate holiday destinations on a globe is a fun way to get them interested and involved in the places you will be travelling to. Vintage toys such as this charming globe and model aeroplanes can be found in street markets like Portobello Road, in London. Previous pages: An endless stretch of desert sand, such as here on the road to the Sossusvlei Sand Dunes in Namibia, promises a once-in-a-lifetime adventure.

journey It is often said that it is not the destination that counts but the journey, but this is a view not generally shared when it comes to travelling with small children. Perhaps we parents don't make the journey the adventure it could be. You may not have had the opportunity when you were young to drive the entire length of Route 66, or follow your favourite football team around Europe, but what is stopping you now? With a little thought and imagination, you can have one holiday experience en route and another on arrival.

A sign on the historic Route 66 near Sedona, Arizona. Once at your destination, a 'telephoto' telescope at the Grand Canyon allows you to frame your favourite view and create a souvenir to take home with you. Opposite: A vintage roadster adds a splash of bright colour to the rural scene. The log cabins in the distance are part of the Stirling Ridge Log Cabin Resort, in Jeffersonville, Vermont.

LAND, SEA AND SKY All aboard the **Arctic Express**, Lapland's only steam train, for two-day excursions in search of Santa Claus • Take a leisurely journey on the **Glacier Express**, the 'slowest fast train in the world', between Zermatt and glamorous St Moritz, with the snow-capped Swiss Alps in the background • The historic railway carriages of **Pullman Railtours** transport guests in style through the White Mountains and Lakes Region of New Hampshire • In Scotland, **Caledonian Macbrayne** offers short ferry hops from Oban to the furthest reaches of the Western Isles, with dolphins and medieval castles to spot along the way • Make like Huckleberry Finn and travel down the Mississippi River on a paddle-wheel steamboat, courtesy of the **Mississippi Queen** • Or take your pick from twelve Mediterranean cruises and set sail aboard the **Queen Victoria**, Cunard's latest cruise ship • The **Skyrail Rainforest Cableway** offers the chance to see the Australian rainforest from a cable car suspended from the world's longest cableway.

open your eyes Sometimes it seems we can't move or think for the images and information fighting for our attention. It is all too easy to succumb to their charms, but the pleasure is fleeting and within a moment we're ready for the next quick fix. What we really want is to be able to return to the awe that comes so naturally to children, to that moment of transfixed wonder that settles upon their little faces on seeing something so utterly new and unexpected. It is a wonderful thing to be able to introduce your child to the great sights, whether a natural spectacle like the Grand Canyon, or a man-made one like the Statue of Liberty. There is so much in our world to see.

The picturesque Monument Valley in the southwestern United States looks straight out of a Wild West film. This national park is part of ancient tribal lands, and is maintained by the Navajo Parks and Recreation Department. A new hotel in this beautiful and evocative landscape, The View Hotel & Spa, will provide guests with a stylish base and feature artwork and jewelry by Native American designers.

UNESCO World Heritage Sites
Of the 851 World Heritage Sites (and counting), these are a few favourites
Angkor Wat, Cambodia
Archaeological Site of Olympia, Greece
Archaeological Site of Troy, Turkey
Buddhist Monuments, Horyu-ji, Japan
Cahokia Mounds State Historic Site, Illinois
Castles and Town Walls of Gwynedd, Wales
Cologne Cathedral, Germany
Dinosaur Provincial Park, Alberta, Canada
Dong Phayayen-Khao Yai Forest Complex, Thailand
Elephant Caves, Mumbai, India
Everglades National Park, Florida
Fatehpur Sikri, Uttar Pradesh, India
Göreme National Park and Cappadocia, Turkey
Grand Canyon, Arizona
Great Barrier Reef, Queensland, Australia
Great Wall of China
Historic Centre of Mexico City, Mexico
Historic Centre of Prague, Czech Republic
Historic Town of St George, Bermuda
Jungfrau-Aletsch-Bietschhorn, Switzerland
Kremlin and Red Square, Moscow, Russia
Kronborg Castle, Island of Sjaelland, Denmark
Liverpool – Maritime Mercantile City, England
Machu Picchu, Peru
Mont-Saint-Michel, Normandy, France
Monticello and the University of Virginia
Naval Port of Karlskrona, Sweden
Old and New Towns of Edinburgh, Scotland
Old Town of Cáceres, Spain
Olympic National Park, Washington
Palace of Diocletian, Split, Croatia
Petra, Jordan
Phong Nha-Ke Bang National Park, Vietnam
Piazza del Duomo, Pisa, Italy
Redwood National and State Parks, California
Samarkand – Crossroads of Cultures, Uzbekistan
Serengeti National Park, Tanzania
Site of Carthage, Tunisia
Skellig Michael, Ireland
Skocjan Caves, Slovenia
Statue of Liberty, New York
Stonehenge, Avebury and Associated Sites, England
Sydney Opera House, Australia
Tikal National Park, Guatemala
Ukhahlamba Drakensberg Park, South Africa
Vallée de Mai Nature Reserve, Seychelles
Victoria Falls, Zambia
Yellowstone National Park, Idaho/Montana

pack Nowadays it seems that we must plan and prepare more than we ever did before. Take a cue from your children and make the preparation a part of the adventure, every bit as exciting as the journey itself. Read stories and study maps together about the places you will visit, and discuss what you might encounter on your travels, from the type of food eaten to customs such as afternoon siestas. Kids can become unsettled by a lack of routine, so it is important to familiarize them with the idea of new things.

Pack cases for children and grown-ups separately. Put into the suitcases the clothes you think you will need, and then take out half and repack; you will still have more than enough.

Vacuum-pack bags will compress clothing, leaving you with fewer cases to pack and carry. And think about using a colour scheme, so you can mix and match with little fuss.

Bring along a disposable camera for the children, digital for you with extra memory card.

A first-aid kit, containing homeopathic remedies, aspirin, insect repellent, digital thermometer, oral rehydration salts, and plasters is an essential.

Sunblock, shampoo, baby wipes and nappies are widely available, so take minimal amounts.

Take a few books, small toys and washable felt-tip pens for younger children, a portable DVD player and an iPod for the older ones.

Only take your child's comfort blanket or toy if you know it can be easily replaced if lost.

If you have infants, take along waterproof sheets to protect hotel beds.

DESTINATION How long is your holiday and what is the best use of your time? • Are you looking for a once-in-a-lifetime trip, or more of the same? • If you want sun and sand, think about places close to you rather than travelling to the other side of the world • Try going out of season: a ski resort without snow might sound odd, but you can still enjoy the stunning views and log cabins at less than half the price • Check travel restrictions and pre-book any kids' clubs or specific places you wish to visit • If you have teenage children, think about inviting their closest friends along to add to the fun • And if anyone in the family has a medical condition, check that help will be readily available, if needed, and keep the packaging of any medicine prescribed abroad • Contact the tourist office for information to share with your children • Consider what your chosen destination offers each member of the family.

BEFORE YOU TRAVEL

Reconfirm travel reservations • Check tourist information websites for any last-minute advice or changes • Ensure everyone has the correct vaccinations • Make sure your hand luggage is prepared for all eventualities • Notebook and a decent travel guide • Essentials in case your suitcase is lost • Boiled sweets for take-off and landing • Plenty of water if travelling by plane (water vapour in the cabin can be as low as 10 to 20 per cent) • PJs for long flights – change the moment you board, so everyone is cosy and comfortable.

DOCUMENTS

An up-to-date passport and international driving licence, if needed • Photocopies of key documents • Bank and credit cards, plus a little local currency to get you from airport to hotel • NHS or insurance cards and copies of medical records • Travel insurance and all emergency numbers • Luggage tags with home and destination addresses • Ribbons or key rings to help make suitcases easily identifiable • Wristbands for the children with your name, mobile number, flight number and destination in case they get lost, even for a moment.

check

CAR

Offering flexibility in location and length of stay, it is no wonder that road trips remain perennially popular • Make sure the car is fully serviced and that the spare tyre is easily accessible and in good condition • Keep an emergency road kit handy, including a torch, blanket, jump leads, rope, pocket knife, duct tape, gloves, tools, extra water and non-perishable snacks • Put heavy items and those you are least likely to need at the bottom of the boot of the car; more frequently needed essentials at the top • Take a cooler bag for snacks and drinks.

HOUSE

Inform a trusted neighbour or a member of the family that you are away and leave them with a set of keys, contact details and an itinerary • Unplug all electrical appliances, except the fridge • Leave plugged in those items connected to timers to give the impression that someone is at home • Ask a young neighbour in need of pocket money to look after the family pets and the garden during your holiday • Alert the post office to hold your mail and your newspaper and/or magazines to suspend subscriptions while you are away.

GAMES

Games on the road do more than amuse the children, they offer the entire family the opportunity to bond and get into the spirit of the adventure • Tell a story about the journey based on exactly where you are at that point • Show younger children how to read maps so they can follow along • When it all gets too much, play a game to see who can be silent the longest • Stop when the children need to stretch their legs and ask them to collect small treasures that catch their eye, which can later be pressed into a scrapbook.

let go of expectations Despite every eventuality planned for and every list made, nature can still surprise you – a storm in the desert, or an absence of snow on the slopes. Expect the unexpected and immerse yourself in the moment. You have nothing but time, so jump in puddles, sing in the rain, wrap the children up in a giant blanket and watch the thunderstorms together from the safety and warmth of the hotel veranda. These are the memories that you will hold dear, when you release any inhibitions and take the time to enjoy what the moment has to offer.

We can all recall *memories* of our first holiday, whether it was a day at the seaside or a summer-long road trip, an unforgettable adventure or a disastrous washout. Every sensation of taste, sight and smell is clear in our minds, and as for the clothes . . . well, we have the pictures to prove we really did wear them! Memories of the family holidays of our childhood will be among our happiest, and it is only natural to wonder how our own children will remember theirs. Will they remember the grand hotels and fine restaurants, or will their memories be about having shared time with family and new friends? Will they recall the life-transforming moments – picking up a lizard for the first time, for example, or seeing a giraffe walking past – or will it be the fussing and fretting over a little cut or graze? Perhaps their memories will be of the beautiful cities they visited, or perhaps they will be clouded by an over-reliance on map-following that overshadowed the joy and spontaneity of the trip. When thinking about the memories we are creating together, the best we can do is to simply relax and enjoy the moment. It is not so much about what we experience, after all, but how we choose to experience it and who we choose to experience it with.

Four generations of the same family on vacation and on the road over three decades in Nebraska, Oregon, Iowa, California, Arizona, Wyoming, Pennsylvania and Illinois. Previous pages: An unexpected rainstorm is cause for a little spontaneous celebration at Frans Indongo Lodge, in Otjiwarongo, Namibia. Overleaf: A tribal keyboard and a hand-stitched toy elephant are among the treasured keepsakes brought back by this little girl from her African holiday.

Part of the *magic* of travelling is coming back with TREASURES we have collected along the way. These m e m e n t o e s aren't the kind of things we can find just anywhere, but are items made by local artisans, using TRADITIONAL skills. Every time we look at them – even years later – we are taken back to that place in *time* and to the people who made them.

local a place in time

unite One of the greatest joys of travelling to different countries is meeting the people who live there. We are eager to learn all about their culture and daily lives, and the ways in which they are different from us – and are perhaps disappointed to find that people aren't so very different after all. Communication needn't require a shared language – more often than not, extravagant gestures and a lot of pointing and smiling will do the trick. Children view every encounter as an opportunity to make a new friend – something that we can all learn from when it comes to living within our own communities.

There is no shortage of playmates at Onguma Bush Camp, in Namibia, and with surroundings like these to explore, children won't miss the lack of a dedicated kids' club. Language differences never seem to faze children: these young guests happily played with their new friends and sang 'Old McDonald's Farm' with the hotel's housekeeper, each in their own language. Overleaf: Time for games and story-telling at Onguma.

city

A visit to the big city – even one close to home – offers a feast for the senses of the young traveller. With so much contrast and variety on offer in a relatively contained area, and new sights and sounds, not to mention a few surprises, around every corner, a day (or a weekend, or even longer) spent in a bustling metropolis is guaranteed to please. Getting the most out of a city break means doing as the locals do, and adapting to the rhythms and routines of your new surroundings. Learn enough of the language to exchange pleasantries, sip a cappuccino in a local café or pick up butter and cheese at a street market, stroll through the winding lanes of an ancient city, stop in at a local church, and haggle just because you can. If your travels take you to Delhi, opt for a white-knuckle ride in a *tuk tuk* alongside the buses, cars and cows jostling for space in the street – no theme park could compete with that! Each city, from the big three of London, Paris and New York to smaller ones around the globe, offers its very own defining experience to be relished, rather than a series of boxes to be ticked.

heritage

Seeing the sights in the great cities of the world

What makes a city a destination? To make it loom large in our imaginations as a place we must visit, at least once in our lives – and once we have, one we want to return to again and again? No doubt part of the appeal lies in the fact that cities are steeped in the history of ages past, with every building and street telling its own story. So many elements combine to define a city, but nothing defines it more than its architecture. High-profile building projects increasingly take their influences from all over the world, but the essential character of any city comes from what is its very own. The canals of Venice, the streets of San Francisco, the boulevards of Paris – all of these immediately give us a sense of place.

Heritage is writ large in the grand monuments of a city. Opposite, left to right: Art Nouveau apartment buildings lining New York's Central Park West; the majestic spires of Hagia Sophia, in Istanbul; a city square overlooked by a graceful statue in mid-flight in Antwerp. Previous pages: Feeding the pigeons in Sanlúcar de Barrameda, in Spain. Pages 36–37: Nothing beats the excitement of seeing a new city for the first time, particularly when it's as beautiful as Venice.

My **gondola** followed the course of the small canals; like the mysterious hand of a genie leading me through the MAZE of this oriental city, they seemed as I advanced, to be carving a road for me through the *heart* of a crowded quarter which they clove asunder, barely dividing with a slender fissure, arbitrarily carved, the tall houses with their tiny Moorish windows; and, as though the *magic* guide had been holding a candle in his hand and were lighting the way for me, they kept casting ahead of them a ray of sunlight for which they carved a path . . .

MARCEL PROUST, *The Sweet Cheat Gone*

A place of turbulent history and incomparable beauty, Venice's appeal to grown-ups needs no explanation, but there is plenty to enthrall younger minds, too. Leave behind the tourist-clogged arteries and head for the less-crowded island of La Giudecca, home to both Harry's Bar (famous for its Bellini cocktails and illustrious patrons like Ernest Hemingway) and Harry's Dolci, which children will love for its gelato and zabaglione. The world-famous Hotel Cipriani and the newer, no less chic Bauer Palladio Hotel & Spa are stylish accommodation choices.

CERAMIC TILES

Ceramic tiles form a colourful decorative backdrop to the Andalucían landscape in Spain. Both practical and beautiful, they are used indoors and out as flooring and to cover fountains (such as in this pretty square). Used inside, the tiles help keep buildings cool during the summer. Patterns and colours are infinitely varied, and cover the design spectrum from geometric to floral. The region's Moorish heritage is visible in its tiles, too, specifically in the brightly coloured *azulejos* with their interlocking patterns.

STREET ART

La Boca is the *barrio* to head to if you find yourself in Buenos Aires and want a taste of the local street-art scene. Located in the southeastern part of the city, near the harbour, the area is popular with tourists for its colourful houses and spontaneous outbreaks of tango; in fact, the variation of the dance called 'Tango Argentino' is thought to have originated here, first performed by the *barrio*'s many Genoese immigrants. La Boca is also home to Boca Juniors, a football team that once boasted Diego Maradona among its players.

place

STONE TEMPLES

The thousand-year-old stone temples of Khajuraho, dedicated to Hindu and Jain deities, are among the most visited tourist destinations in India. Located in the region of Madhya Pradesh, Khajuraho is about 620 kilometres southeast of Delhi; the temples themselves cover an area of 21 square kilometres, with carvings that are still crisply visible and cover the monuments in their entirety. The temples are divided into three groups (western, eastern and southern), with Kandariya Mahadeo the largest temple of them all.

WOODEN HOUSES

Painted wooden houses were once a common sight in Istanbul, but have in recent years fallen into decay. Built primarily in the late 19th century, these structures consist of the earlier *konak*, or stand-alone house, and the row house. Visitors who wish to step back in time should head to Ayranci Sokagi, a well-preserved Ottoman neighbourhood that has retained its old houses. And you can even stay in them: a row of nine wooden houses forms the Ayasofya Pansiyonlari, a pensione standing in the shadow of Istanbul's great mosque, Hagia Sophia.

PAINTED DOORWAYS

Colourful painted doorways are a feature of Tangier's narrow streets, which continually teem with locals and tourists. The harbour town of Tangier, one of Morocco's largest cities, has its edginess, but there is plenty for families to enjoy. A must is a stop at the town's *medina*, or marketplace, where bargaining is the way to get your shopping done. Tangier also has quick connections by train to some of the region's other great cities: Casablanca, Marrakech, Fès. The beach, pedestrian areas and gardens have all benefited from recent makeovers.

sightseeing There was a time in our lives when seeing the sights meant sitting all night in a smoky jazz club, lingering over umpteen coffees or cocktails, or spending hours sifting through boxes of vinyl in a record shop. This was the cool way to see a city, and the idea of visiting Times Square filled us with dread. But the tourist destinations are an important part of a city's identity, and a child's delight in visiting them brings its own, equally sweet reward. It's never too late to experience the thrill of seeing the neon signs on 42nd Street, a water taxi passing in front of the Statue of Liberty, or the iconic Brooklyn Bridge – this time through the eyes of your children. Who knows, you might even enjoy it.

The bright lights of Hong Kong's splendidly modern skyline, seen from the Kowloon Peninsula. Those wishing for the same viewing experience can catch the Star Ferry at Edinburgh Place, and ride across Victoria Harbour out to Kowloon; the ferry also travels to Central Side. Panoramic views can be seen from the top of Victoria Peak, too, which can be reached by tram. Once in the city, children will want to pay a visit to the Lam Tsuen Wishing Tree, next to the Tin Hau temple: wishes are written onto a red slip of paper (available from one of the many nearby stalls), and then tied

onto an orange with string. The oranges are then tossed up into the tree; if they hook onto a branch the wish will come true, and they it catch at the very top of the tree, it will come true even sooner. Next might be a visit to Stanley Market, which sells all manner of trinkets and souvenirs, as well as arts and crafts and designer goods. Once you have tired of shopping, the market also has a beach for sunbathing and a host of riverside restaurants and bars, as well as an 18th-century temple.

SKYSCRAPERS

Skyscrapers are reaching ever-more impressive heights these days, with even the towers at Kuala Lumpur being outstripped by the continuous building projects in Dubai. But New York is the city most associated with skyscrapers, from the Art Déco General Electric Tower (seen right) to the Flatiron Building on Broadway and the Chrysler Building in Midtown, to the majestic apartment blocks of the Upper West Side. Visitors to the city can take a lift to the top of the granddaddy of them all, the 102-storey Empire State Building.

RAILWAY STATIONS

All aboard! The much-anticipated new Eurostar terminal has finally opened at London's St Pancras Station, located between King's Cross and Euston. Passengers will now travel to Paris and other destinations, such as Lille and Brussels, from the cavernous terminal located behind the historic Midlands Grand Hotel, itself undergoing a massive refit. The Eurostar terminal has a large retail space, featuring specialty food shops and the world's longest Champagne bar. Below: Another great landmark, New York's Grand Central Station.

icons

GRAND FAÇADES

The iron-and-glass main railway station in Antwerp provides a fittingly grand welcome to the city. Designed by Louis Delacenserie in 1905 and considered Belgium's finest example of railway architecture, Antwerpen Centraal underwent a major refurbishment in 1998, and high-speed trains are due to begin departing from the station within the year. Also in and around Koningin Astridplein is a diamond museum, a zoo, and the Designcenter de Winkelhaak – an exhibition space, workshop and showcase for local design.

BRIDGES

Can there be any more iconic structure than the Brooklyn Bridge? Connecting the New York boroughs of Manhattan and Brooklyn, construction work began on the bridge in 1870 (finishing in 1883), and it has loomed large in the American consciousness ever since. The bridge has featured in film (*Saturday Night Fever*), television (*The Cosby Show*), and song (*Monty Python's Flying Circus*), as well as more literary fare. A walk across the bridge on a sunny day into Brooklyn for brunch is a brilliant way to spend a weekend morning.

MUSEUMS

'Not *another* museum!' is a plaintive cry often heard by city-visiting parents with their young charges in tow. But the Museum of Modern Art in New York is something special. All the greatest hits of contemporary art are here for the parents, including Van Gogh's *Starry Night*, as well as a chic, revamped café. To make the visit even more enjoyable for kids, the museum has two websites geared to the younger visitor: 'Destination Modern Art' for children aged 5 to 8, and 'Red Studio' for those who are a little older.

storybooks We all remember the best-loved stories of our childhood, and remember, too, the thrill of visiting cities that were new to us and home to our favourite characters. Children today are just the same, and will delight in visiting Eloise's Plaza Hotel in New York and Madeline's Paris – or even Harry Potter's railway platform! It is exciting for children to the see the places of their imagination become real, and wonderful for parents to see their offspring engaging with the written word.

On the long platform at King's Cross Station in London, it is easy to believe that the Hogwarts Express has just arrived, ready to take passengers back to school for a new year of adventures. Opposite: A sign on the wall marks the spot where Harry and his friends make the leap to Platform 9¾. Here, two visitors try to do the same! Previous pages: The Eiffel Tower (left) and the London Eye (right) light up the night sky.

BOOKS IN THE CITY Favourite characters have been immortalized in sculpture throughout the world • Mrs Mallard and her eight ducklings take a stroll in **Boston**'s Public Garden (*Make Way for Ducklings*, Robert McCloskey) • Alice hosts a tea party in **New York**'s Central Park (*Alice's Adventures in Wonderland*, Lewis Carroll) • In **London**, Peter Pan is poised for flight in Kensington Gardens (*Peter Pan*, J.M. Barrie) and Paddington Bear sits patiently with his suitcase at Paddington Station (*A Bear Called Paddington*, Michael Bond) • The Little Mermaid keeps watch over **Copenhagen**'s harbour (*The Little Mermaid*, Hans Christian Andersen) • Greyfriars Bobby does the same in **Edinburgh** (*Greyfriars Bobby*, Lavinia Derwent) • Henry, Ribsy and Ramona liven up Grant Park in **Portland, Oregon** (*Henry Huggins*, Beverly Cleary).

museums A visit to a museum needn't be a dull and stuffy day out. When the building itself is as unusual as the Guggenheim, sometimes – especially with very young children – that is all you need. For older kids, museums provide a window onto a city's heritage and a peek into the lives of past residents. From the small, local historical societies to the cavernous treasure-filled palaces to art, museums introduce children to the wider world.

The unmistakable – and unmissable – ramps of Frank Lloyd Wright's Guggenheim Museum in New York frame a unique space in which to learn about art, architecture and the great monuments of a great city.

inspire Make the most of an outing to the big city by relating it to your child's interests and hobbies. Perhaps a famous footballer is known to have visited a certain restaurant, or perhaps a favourite author or person from history lived nearby. Whatever the reason, city visits are more meaningful when your children's curiosity is engaged: their desire to see where Princess Diana lived may have brought you to London's Kensington Palace, for example, or taken you to Rome because that is where pasta is made. Plan activities that include these youthful passions, from a visit to your local Natural History Museum to see the dinosaurs, perhaps, to a trip to an open-air ice rink in the courtyard of an historic building.

An outing to London's Somerset House for a turn around the ice-skating rink is a special treat. Children who love history will adore learning about the building's previous royal residents, art lovers will gravitate to The Courtauld Gallery (also on the premises), and parents will appreciate the tent serving hot apple cider and more fortifying beverages. The ice rink is open during the winter months only, November through January.

Time reserved for just you and your child is a cause for *celebration*. Make the day a true occasion by doing something together that is a little bit SPECIAL, like taking afternoon tea in a grand city hotel. This is a chance for your child to dress up in *mummy's* pearls and for both of you to share a grown-up moment that will be **cherished** and remembered for years to come.

occasion another world

CAVALIERI HILTON, ROME

Experience a little of *la dolce vita* at this lovely hotel perched atop the highest of Rome's seven hills. The three-Michelin-starred restaurant La Pergola is here, with its stunning views over St Peter's basilica and the Vatican in the distance, as is the Lobby Bar for afternoon tea or a cocktail under the palm trees, and the Terrazza del Giardino dell'Uliveto, a charming poolside café offering candlelit dinners against a backdrop of live music. The Cavalieri Hilton is a truly elegant and stylish introduction to Italy's Eternal City.

THE FOUR SEASONS, NEW YORK

It's hard to imagine a hotel that does more to epitomize the local attitude to stylish luxury than The Four Seasons. This I.M. Pei-designed building houses many a must-visit dining destination, including L'Atelier de Joël Robuchon, featuring a nightly *menu dégustation*; The Bar, popular for after-hours martinis; and TY in the lobby for afternoon tea. Barney's and Bergdorf Goodman are steps away, and a concierge is on hand to help direct families to such sights as the Metropolitan Museum of Art and South Street Seaport.

hotels

MANDARIN ORIENTAL, HONG KONG

Built in the 1960s, the Mandarin Oriental in Hong Kong has seen its fair share of illustrious visitors: Princess Diana, Tom Cruise, and several US presidents have all stayed here. More humble visitors will find plenty to occupy them, too, as the hotel has no fewer than ten restaurants and bars on its premises, including Pierre Gagnaire's eponymous eatery and The Chinnery, a British-themed club with a vast selection of malt whiskies. Among the nearby attractions are the Maritime Museum and Hong Kong Disneyland.

THE BERKELEY, LONDON

In the heart of Knightsbridge, The Berkeley whisks visitors back to a civilized age of fine dining and cocktails. Formerly located near Berkeley Square, the hotel's reputation was such that its restaurant was one of the few places where debutantes could socialize unchaperoned. Today's stylish diners vie for tables at Gordon Ramsay's Boxwood Café or the distinctly stylish Blue Bar. The Berkeley also hosts 'fashion teas', featuring cakes and petits-fours inspired by the season's fashion collections, and a special tea on Mothering Sunday.

HÔTEL DE CRILLON, PARIS

Home to the many-starred restaurant, Les Ambassadeurs, and the site of the annual *bal des débutantes*, the Crillon is a destination for special occasions. Designed in 1758 by Jacques-Ange Gabriel, acquired by the Comte de Crillon in 1788 and in the Crillon family for the next 119 years, the hotel boasts a history as distinguished as its location overlooking the place de la Concorde and steps from the elegant rue du Faubourg St-Honoré. The Louvre is nearby, as is the Café Marly, a sophisticated spot for a cocktail.

urban village

Exploring a city's unique neighbourhoods

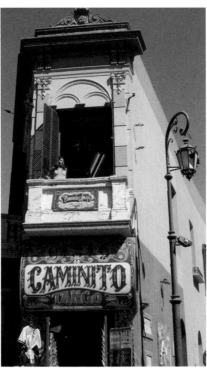

The big sights and tourist draws certainly have their attractions, but it is in the urban villages that the beating heart of any city is to be found. When visiting these local neighbourhoods, it's much more rewarding to step off the tour bus, or emerge from the subway, and instead start exploring the city streets on foot. The character and personality of the individual areas and their residents immediately becomes more apparent, and your visit richer and more memorable. You may not find the biggest museums or the smartest restaurants in the urban villages, but you will stumble across the street markets, speciality boutiques and tiny thoroughfares that make these little enclaves so unique.

Urban villages are to be found all over the world. Opposite, left to right: In London, Portobello Road's quirky shopfronts and stalls add to the funky feel of the Notting Hill neighbourhood. La Boca, a barrio in Buenos Aires, is famous for its street entertainers, festive atmosphere and spontaneous outbreaks of tango, whereas New York's highly charged, individual character can be seen even in corporate Midtown.

getting around Whether a yellow cab, a rickshaw, bicycle or gondola, whatever you choose, most cities have safe and inexpensive forms of transport that not only get you to where you are going, but form an integral part of the city experience. Choose to see a city from the top of a double-decker bus or the glass-covered deck of a *bateau mouche*, or in a *tuk tuk* clattering along narrow lanes – while at the same time not forgetting to partake in a few of the old clichés, like taking a horse and carriage around Central Park or a cable car up and down the thrillingly steep streets of San Francisco. In the Low Countries, a bicycle is the transport of choice.

The best way to get around Bruges is by bicycle. Bring your own, or rent them at the railway station or in one of the many nearby cycle shops. A 'bicycle combination ticket' includes the rental of a bicycle for a full day, admission to three museums of your choice, and a drink in the Folklore Museum's De Zwarte Kat. Tickets are available at local museums or the Hotel Koffieboontje. Overleaf: The bright lights and big sounds of Manhattan.

stop information overload

Stop, go, slow down, look both ways – rules make us feel *safe* when we encounter the unfamiliar, but too many commands can be overwhelming. As parents, we need to take a *check* on how much of what we say is necessary and how much is nagging, and to recognize the difference. While holidays are time for a little rule-breaking, once the new boundaries have been established, just slow down the PACE and *enjoy* the moment.

Clearing one's throat loudly in China is considered vulgar, but in Arabic countries, go right ahead.

Say *pardon* whenever you get in someone's way in France. Tips are not expected for taxi rides.

In India, the constant beeping of horns does not mean that you are in the way, drivers do it to tell you that they will be! When taking a cab, always ask the price first and bargain.

You will find that in Mexico people get very close to your space in conversation, but refrain from drawing back as this would cause offence.

When visiting churches in Italy, be sure to cover your shoulders and knees. Just keep a cardigan, or better still a light shawl, with you at all times.

Visitors to Venice won't need to think too hard about the rules of street etiquette as the city has thoughtfully posted signs everywhere to remind you.

In Buenos Aires, you will be drawn to the spontaneous outbreaks of tango taking place on the little streets. Smile and nod, but never give the 'thumb's up' or OK sign, as both are deemed rude.

Be careful about crossing the road at undesignated points in the US; in some states, 'jaywalking' is a misdemeanour.

exploring on foot If time and energy levels allow, the best way by far to see any city is by foot. Walking allows you to see so much more of the many urban villages that make up any grand city, and there is less chance of missing those hidden cafés or speciality shops. And there's the added pleasure of stopping at whatever entices and indulging in a local souvenir, like having a Bollywood-style poster painted of the children, or a bindi stuck to your forehead. It's amazing how far children will walk on holiday without complaining — they are far too busy taking it all in to notice the distances.

There is no end to the sights you will see when taking in a country as diverse as India by foot. Here, children enjoy the universal game of tag in Varanasi (formerly known as Benares). Opposite: A holy man takes a rest in Orcha, while a camel named Raj earns his living by giving rides to tourists. The giant bunnies are bred by locals in Manali, known as India's 'honeymoon capital' as so many Bollywood movies are filmed there. Previous pages: A little girl finds an alternative means of transport in the La Boca barrio of Buenos Aires.

parks Like green oases of tranquillity in a sea of grey concrete, parks
are where city dwellers go to breathe. The moment you step into one,
you can feel the pace of life slow down and your stress levels decline.
Parks are a great place in which to soak up the energy of a city, where
grown-ups take time out for a lunch break, children play and feed the ducks,
and everyone relaxes. Even the world's great parks – from Central Park to
Hampstead Heath – have a neighbourly feel to them, just like the one
down your own road.

*A snowy day doesn't deter visitors to Hampstead Heath, in North London, while in Paris a passerby finds
a restful spot near Les Halles. Opposite: Frederick Law Olmsted's Central Park is beloved of New Yorkers
and visitors alike. Here, picnickers enjoy a quiet patch of grass on the edge of the Boat Lake and the views
of the apartment blocks of the Upper East Side.*

WHERE TO FIND THEM Located just outside **London**, Richmond Park (Henry VIII's former hunting grounds) covers 2,000 acres •
Be sure not to miss the Japanese tea gardens or an opera performance at the open-air amphitheatre in **San Francisco**'s Golden Gate
Park • Next to the Royal Palace in the centre of **Stockholm**, Kungsträdgården is home to restaurants and an ice-skating rink • The
recently renovated Christopher Columbus Park is the place to watch the boats in **Boston**'s harbour • Centennial Park in **Sydney** is
where Aussies catch a film at the outdoor moonlight cinema • Larger than Manhattan's Central Park, Phoenix Park in **Dublin** is home
to a herd of wild deer • Flower-lovers should head to **Singapore**'s Botanic Garden for its over 60,000 varieties of orchids.

local eats While every city will have its themed restaurants,
the food in these places can often be disappointing and the whole
experience rather dull. It is much more exciting to stumble upon
a nearby trattoria, or to seek out little gems recommended by
locals. Such restaurants offer the ideal venue in which children can
discover new tastes for themselves, and are just as much about the
local attitude to children. 'One cannot think well, love well, sleep
well, if one has not dined well,' said Virginia Woolf – words for
everyone to travel by, indeed.

*Chocolate, moules frites and pretzels are always welcome favourites with young travellers.
Opposite: This restaurant in Antwerp is the perfect spot for pommes frites, eaten the Belgian
way with mayonnaise. Overleaf: A young gourmand finds a treat in the window of The
Hummingbird Bakery, in London's Portobello Road.*

WHAT TO TRY When in **Italy**, try ice cream as it was meant to be; the *gelato* at Nannini in Siena is revered by many as the best • It will
be easy to appease young and picky appetites in **France** with all the delicious cheese, fresh bread and pastries on offer • **Maine** is the place
for lobster, especially when eaten the traditional way – at a beachside clambake • Clam chowder in a bowl made from sourdough bread is
always a favourite in **San Francisco**, and even better when enjoyed within sight of the Golden Gate Bridge • In **London**, a serving of fish
and chips wrapped in newspaper is ideal for a quick lunch; the Sea Shell in Marylebone is handy for Madame Tussaud's and Regent's Park •
When in **Spain**, do as the Spaniards do and tuck into multiple small dishes of *tapas* – then hurl your olive pips and napkins to the floor! •
Greek food, with all the yoghurt- and lamb-based dishes, is easy for children to manage – and healthy for them, too • Head to Restaurant
Praq just outside **Amsterdam** for a fun restaurant where children have their own special seating area.

Soon her eye fell on a little glass box
that was lying under the table: she opened
it, and found in it a very small *cake*,
on which the words 'EAT ME' were
beautifully marked in currants . . .

LEWIS CARROLL, *Alice's Adventures in Wonderland*

treats   something sweet

markets Alive with the sounds of local voices and the sights of food, furniture, flowers, and everything in between, street markets are a vivid lesson in what is truly unique about the cities we visit. The different ways in which stallholders and their customers communicate, too, allow us a glimpse into a city's culture that is both immediate and resonating. Bartering in a Moroccan *souk* or a Turkish bazaar with all the lanterns turned on and the smell of spices in the air, for example, is a shopping experience like no other. And in a world that looks increasingly identical from one place to the next, the unique character of a street market is a welcome departure from the usual sterile shopping mall.

Portobello Road's market is world-famous, and sells an astonishing variety of goods and antiques along its crowded pavements. What can be more fun than trying on sunglasses and a cowboy hat, and asking a local bobby for directions? The child-friendly S&M Café is a favourite with kids for its endless combinations of sausage and mash, as is Honey Jam for its nostalgic toys. Overleaf: Some of the sights along Portobello Road, including The Red Teapot Arcade.

STREET MARKETS The Christkindelsmärik in **Strasbourg** is the biggest and the oldest Christmas market, in business since 1570 • For flowers, be sure not to miss **Amsterdam**'s Bloemenmarkt, a floating market on the Singel with its flower stalls on houseboats • The Grand Bazaar in **Istanbul** is the place for haggling, Eastern-style, and for coming away with a rug or two • The Antique Market located in the historic Randolph Street area of **Chicago** features a Junior Collectors' Club • Saturday Market in **Portland, Oregon** is a West Coast institution, and features goods made by local artisans, plus two stages for music and performances • For a true market adventure, this one in the mountains of **Otavalo, Ecuador** sells crafts made by the local Otavaleño people • Marché aux Puces in **Paris**, often described as the biggest flea-market in the world, has everything from Art Déco lighting fixtures to garden furniture on offer.

FOOD MARKETS In the shadow of Southwark Cathedral, a fruit and vegetable market has been trading in the Borough area of **London** since before the Romans arrived • Now covered by Enric Miralles' striking roof, the famous La Boqueria in **Barcelona** dates back to the 13th century • The beloved 'greenmarket' in **New York**'s Union Square sells plants alongside farm-sourced produce and cheese • It's all about the fish at Pike Place Market in **Seattle**, and no visit is complete without a latte at the original Starbucks and a bowl of clam chowder at nearby Ivar's • A visit to any one of the many neighbourhood food markets in **Paris** is a must; try those on the rue Mouffetard and the rue Montorgueil. Above: All kinds of goods sure to appeal to the discerning shopper are lovingly displayed in Nice, France. Opposite: Markets provide local services as well as food, such as here in El Puerto de Santa María, in Spain.

festival

Occasions for celebrating, wherever you travel

Christmas in Iceland or New Year in China – you need not go far to enjoy such experiences, as the diverse cultural mix of any great city will offer these celebrations, and more, closer to home. Such occasions show us the city with its volume turned up: a moving, living theatre on the streets where there is drama, adventure, music, food, and people revelling in the joy of the moment. What could be more entertaining for a child than the firecracker of surprises offered by a large- or smaller-scale festival? Consider timing a city break to coincide with a local holiday; many such festivals will have children's days, and the fun and excitement will be as much for you as it is for them.

This little girl is ready for celebrating in her grown-up party dress. Pretty native costumes, such as this one from Spain, are more beautiful and longer lasting than the polyester, over-priced creations on sale at your nearby party goods store, and are a wonderful keepsake to pass on to younger siblings or to treasure for one's own.

holi This Hindu festival celebrates the coming of spring in a joyous explosion of colour. Kicked off with a bonfire, the celebrations really get underway with the ritual throwing of powdered pigment over everyone and everything in your path. When better than when the Earth renews itself to let yourself go in a dizzying ecstasy of release? Later, participants – washed and renewed themselves – attend parties where sweets are served to represent the sweetness in nature.

At this Holi celebration in Orcha, the children's shorts and T-shirts (white cotton is traditionally worn during the festivities) were made out of hotel pillowcases supplied by the proprietor. The paint-covered pillowcases came home with the family after their travels and are now framed and hanging on the wall. Overleaf: Colourful lanterns in Hong Kong mark another festive occasion.

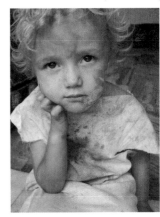

Chance encounters can often be the most rewarding. We learn from the sights and sounds of places that are new to us, but the MEMORIES that linger long after the holiday is over are often the ones we have of the people we met along the way. In the past, it was a *courtesy* to doff your hat to a stranger, but today's children are too often taught to be fearful of extending even the most basic of *pleasantries*.

contact brief encounter

CINCO DE MAYO

Originally a Mexican holiday to celebrate the Battle of Puebla in 1862, Cinco de Mayo (Fifth of May) has become a day that honours Mexican–American heritage and is celebrated primarily in the United States, particularly in the Southwest. Food, music and dance are the order of the day, while schoolchildren mark the occasion by bashing piñatas with a stick to unleash a torrent of candy. Cities and regions with strong Mexican ties, such as Los Angeles and California's Central Valley, are good places to join in the festivities.

FIREWORKS

A national holiday is always a joyous cause for celebration, and even better if you happen to be there for it. Watching parades and fireworks (from a safe distance) can instantly make you feel a part of the community you are visiting, and it is a wonderful opportunity to tuck into regional dishes with the locals and taste something new. Some national holidays to catch are Australia Day (26 January), National Foundation Day in Japan (11 February), St David's Day in Wales (1 March), Canada Day (1 July), and Bastille Day in France (14 July).

celebrate

NOTTING HILL CARNIVAL

Forty years on and still going strong, the Notting Hill Carnival, held over the August Bank Holiday weekend, is a date in every Londoner's diary – along with those of plenty of visitors. Originally conceived as a way to celebrate the largely Caribbean heritage of the area's residents, today the festival is a multi-cultural extravaganza. Brightly decorated floats, children in equally bright costumes, food stands and music all contribute to the heady party atmosphere. For visiting children, this is a great introduction to the colourful melting pot that is London.

PUERTO RICAN DAY

Those who have spent any time at all living in New York know that every June traffic and all other activity comes to a halt as Manhattanites, visitors and Puerto Ricans alike turn out in droves to celebrate the commonwealth's national day. The parade route winds its festive way up Fifth Avenue from 44th Street, before turning east into 86th Street. Local celebrities with Puerto Rican links are often invited to act as the parade's Grand Marshal. Colour, music, dancing, food, noise and entertainment: the Puerto Rican Day parade has it all.

RELIGIOUS FESTIVALS

Attending services or celebrations of another culture's religious festivals can be a moving experience or an exhilaratingly joyful one, as with the Hindu festival of Holi (see pages 88–89). Despite their often sombre meanings, religious holidays can be fun for visiting children, too. The festival of *Los Tres Reyes Magos* in Spain, which takes place on 5 January, involves gifts for children, parades and fireworks; it is followed the next day by *Día de los Reyes*, or Epiphany (right). Opposite: a young reveller at the Notting Hill Carnival.

holy places Every concentration of people – from the largest city to the humblest of villages – has its centres of worship, and no matter one's religious persuasion, it is fascinating for children to observe the different customs and traditions associated with the places they visit. Participating in small ways, from lighting a candle in a side chapel to tucking a posy of flowers into a shrine at the side of the road, is a valuable lesson in respect for children, and engages their interest in the lives of people beyond their own experience. Holy places are also all about welcoming visitors into the community; at the Golden Temple in the Punjab, India, volunteers feed each one of the forty thousand visitors that pass through its doors every day.

Incense sticks and other offerings decorate this temple in Hong Kong. Opposite: Spiritual moments can happen in the unlikeliest places, such as in this Spanish hotel, a former monastery near the Portuguese border, where simple furnishings and monumental candlesticks add to the sombre mood. Pages 92–93: This sleepy village of white-washed houses and narrow streets is Vejer de la Frontera, in Andalucía, Spain.

adventure

Not a moment passes without our taking a breath, yet months can go by without our taking the time to appreciate nature in all its awe-inspiring glory. Whether star-gazing from a sleeping bag on the ground or hurtling down a mountain on a pair of skis, adventure holidays allow us to widen our horizons and spend time in the great outdoors, and to experience what it is to truly breathe. Exhilarating, exciting and fun, they also give us the opportunity to be children again, and take us back to a time when we would try anything, regardless of the fear. However frightening or daunting it may seem, taking ourselves out of our comfort zones will do wonders for the soul, and there is no better way to encourage children to be courageous than to see their parents doing the same. A little adventure and daring gives children the ability to sharpen both mind and body, and teamwork for the sake of a common goal leaves both children and parents with an invaluable sense of achievement.

land

Holidays close to the Earth, connecting us to the land

'Study nature, love nature, stay close to nature' – so Frank Lloyd Wright first urged his students over half a century ago, and his words still resonate today. Children first learn to associate security and safety with the family, later acquiring the confidence to expand their circle of social interaction. But beyond this, they have a real need to feel a connection to the land if they are to flourish into compassionate, intelligent beings. The very act of planting a seed and watching it grow, or letting the soil run through our fingers, shows us just how much a part of the Earth we are. We may have forgotten how much joy and contentment comes from being immersed in nature, but for children, it is the most natural place to be.

The wide open spaces and scrubland of the Namibian landscape reinforce our connection to the outdoors. Here, a young guest strolls in the bush near Etosha National Park. Previous pages: The rugged natural beauty of Twyfelfontein, in Namibia's Damaraland. Pages 98–99: En route from Mowani Mountain Camp to the Sossusvlei Sand Dunes, stopping off near Swakopmund, a former German colonial outpost founded in 1892.

camping Travelling within our own country and setting up camp along the way has become an increasingly appealing option for the globally aware, anxious to leave behind as minimal a carbon footprint as possible. But even when venturing further afield, camping in the outdoors offers an attractive mix of flexibility and freedom in choosing where to camp for the night and where to head to next. It also allows us to base ourselves close to a chosen activity – whether tackling a mountain pass in the Himalayas (below) or the surf in Wales (opposite) – and the chance to make new friends with fellow campers and adventurers, wherever those adventures might take us.

A camping holiday in the Indian Himalayas. Open from May to November, the Rohtang Pass has a fearsome reputation stemming from its name – 'rohtang' means 'pile of corpses' in Persian! This family has nothing to fear, however, as the region is a popular tourist destination with plenty of guides available for hire in Manali, about 51 kilometres away. Opposite: The adventure continues in Pembrokeshire, where the children are ready to try their hand at surfing off the South Wales coast.

GETTING STARTED Be realistic about your needs when planning where to camp – is the luxury of a toilet close by more important than a view? • Bring lots of layers for bedding (silk liners, sleeping bags, duvets and sheepskin for extra warmth) and air it daily to ensure your confined space feels clean and comfortable • Take along plenty of loose, warm clothing, as well as walking shoes and wellies • Camping offers a great sense of community, all the more reason to choose a child-friendly site • If it is your first time, don't go anywhere too remote, as you will doubtless want some help putting up the tent and lighting your first fire • When arriving at a site, opt for a shady area on level ground, as this will offer the best protection from sun and rain • A bucket is much more than a bucket – it's also an invaluable tool for washing, carrying firewood, and upending for an extra stool • Be sure to bring a torch for each child and one for adults (practical and all part of the fun); jam jars filled with tea lights for night-time magic; twine for shelters, washing lines and kites; old picnic blankets that can double up as bedding • Leave your inhibitions at home as this is the perfect time for singing and story-telling with the little ones.

under the stars For those unconvinced by the full outdoor adventure, a home-made tent in the garden allows the whole family to experience the wonder of seeing the stars together. We can all recall our first experience of sleeping outdoors, playing hide-and-seek in and around the tent, arranging our family of dollies and soft toys, and reading by torchlight. Fortunately for us, rediscovering this simplest of pleasures is a lot more comfortable than we might imagine.

MAKE A TENT IN YOUR GARDEN

Visit your local 'Little India' (like Brick Lane in London, or nearby Southall) or textile market • Take three saris of 6 metres each, and cut them in half lengthwise to give you six panels • Stitch the panels together, also lengthwise, to make one large curtain • Bunch the fabric together at one end and fasten using a decorative cord or ribbon • Stitch a hanging cord to the centre of the bunched fabric, and attach to a hoop, 1 metre in diameter • Hang from a tree branch in the garden • Just add a guitar, a torch, and a family of treasured toys, and you'll have all the adventure you need.

A caravan nestles under the trees at the Manorowen Walled Garden, near the coastal town of Fishguard, in Pembrokeshire. This one-and-a half acre kitchen garden dates back to the 18th century, and is an inviting place for a spot of rest and relaxation in a sylvan setting. The garden's staff, too, can put their feet up, as the caravan provides a convenient shelter for their tea breaks. Sights such as this little garden are wonderful places to stop at and explore while on a camping holiday, places we might otherwise miss if travelling by more conventional means. This family pitched up

at Whitesands Beach, a popular surfing destination at the end of St David's peninsula, in South Wales. Campsites near tourist activities – such as surfing at Whitesands – will more often than not have a café or farmers' market close at hand, but you may still want to bring along the basics for a picnic, including plastic plates, cutlery and tumblers, as well as a bread knife, tin opener, and salt and pepper. Not forgetting, of course, the all-important corkscrew!

riding No matter what your riding adventure involves – whether horses, camels, or even elephants – it is the sheer height of these animals that is their best advantage as far as children are concerned. The benefits of horseback riding for disabled children, or hippotherapy, have also been recognized. The gentle, rocking movement of a horse's gait encourages good posture by engaging core muscles to work together to keep the rider upright, and the animal's body temperature (a horse's is higher than that of a human's) is soothing and comforting. Riding creates a real sense of achievement, independence and self-confidence – a bonus for any child.

A horseback riding adventure at The Desert Homestead and Horsetrails, in Maerua Park, Namibia. Visitors to the homestead can choose from a variety of activities, including the Sunrise Ride, where guests set off at dawn across the African bush before arriving a lavish picnic spread, set up on tables underneath one of the region's characteristic Camelthorn trees. The friendly staff entertain visiting children with stories, and sing traditional folk tunes to diners in the evening over supper. Overleaf: A riding excursion gets underway at The Desert Homestead.

RIDES OF A LIFETIME Follow the 'Adventure Ranch' trail on horseback at Whistler, **Canada**'s world-famous ski resort, in view of Mt Currie • In **Texas**, learn the ropes at a real dude ranch where cowboys and the rugged landscape provide the backdrop to a holiday on horseback for the adventurous • Join a sheep round-up in **Iceland** while riding on native ponies through deep blankets of snow and across frozen lakes • **Indonesia** is the perfect destination for rides along the beach at sunset, stopping at local villages along the way • When in **England**, try your hand at hacking across the Lakeland Fells, the home of Beatrix Potter and Peter Rabbit and to some of the UK's most traditionally beautiful countryside • The Camargue, a southern region in **France** on the edge of the Mediterranean, offers the chance to ride along canals and the forested banks of the Rhône • Experience Big Sky Country on horseback – **Montana**'s renowned rivers, creeks and streams offer a great opportunity to hop off your horse and try a spot of fly-fishing.

agritourism In marked contrast to the usual hotel experience, holidays spent on a working farm allow travellers the chance to share meals with the family and farm hands, and to help out with chores, from milking the cows in the morning to collecting eggs from the hen house and apples from the orchard. We all learn by doing, and getting a little dirty every once in a while does nobody any harm. Vacations like these also give children a better understanding of nature's life cycles and where food comes from, as well as a valuable lesson in how enriching it is to live without waste.

A country farm provides all the fixings for a hearty meal. Here at Valley Dream Farm, near Cambridge, Vermont, all of the produce is certified organic. Vegetables and other crops are available, as are hanging baskets, flowers, herbs and bedding plants.

ORGANIC FARMS IN THE USA At **The Inn at Celebrity Dairy**, a working dairy in Chatham County, North Carolina, breakfast is taken with the farm hands, and Sunday dinner is a celebratory event featuring the dairy's own cheese • **Inn Serendipity** is a bed-and-breakfast outside Monroe, Wisconsin that prides itself on leading the way in energy conservation and environmentally and socially responsible living • **The Philo Apple Farm** is an organic farm in California's scenic Mendocino County that has it all: cottages for paying guests, a farmstand selling own-grown produce, as well as a cooking school • Bird watching, horseback riding, or just hanging out with the sheep are all on offer at **Lavender Hill Farm** in Virginia's Shenandoah Valley • **Liberty Hill Farm** in the Green Mountains of Vermont is an 1825 farmhouse that features country breakfasts and a 'cheese trail' • As well as producing a magazine, the organic **Mary Jane's Farm** in Moscow, Idaho offers a variety of activities, including the Pay Dirt Farm School • **North Country Farm,** located well and truly away from the city bustle on the Hawaiian island of Kauai, offers two bed-and-breakfast cottages and encourages guests to pick vegetables from the garden.

All shapes of **beauty**, grace
and strength, all hues we know,
Green blades of grass and warbling
birds, children that gambol and play,
the clouds of *heaven* above . . .

Walt Whitman, *Proud Music of the Storm*

farm

sowing the seeds

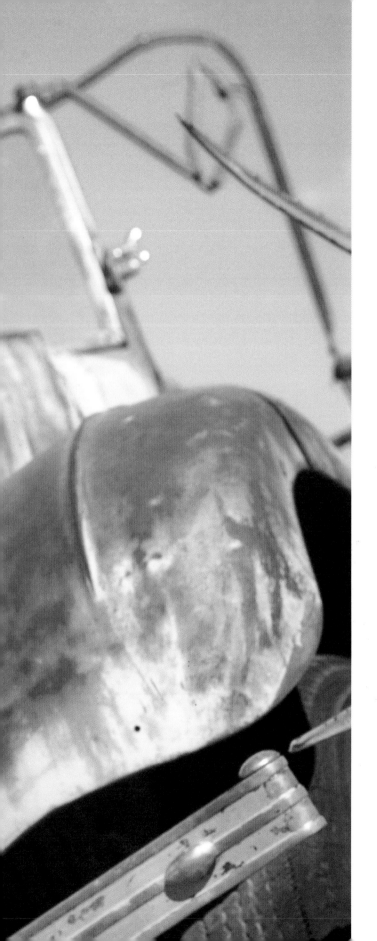

road trip   Plane travel can leave the rather unsettling feeling of having been abruptly dropped somewhere, quite literally out of the sky. You have arrived in a different place, with different smells and sounds, not to mention a different time zone, and are probably exhausted and disoriented, without the time (despite the hours spent in the air) to adjust to your new surroundings. Travelling by car, on the other hand, provides a much gentler way of arriving at one's destination. It is more natural and satisfying to arrive slowly – a bit like our romantic idea of gypsies in their caravans – and there is the added pleasure of experiencing the countryside unfolding. Best of all, road trips create an intimate connection with the land you are passing through.

On the way from Mowani Mountain Camp to the Sossusvlei Sand Dunes, in Namibia. After spending hours on the road with nothing but dry land in sight, this little boy and his family came across a burnt-out car and – more surprisingly – a small shack with Hershey bars in the fridge, Hello magazine on the table, and Manchester United on the telly.

on the road Children will enjoy long hours spent in the car so much more if they are made part of the adventure. Older children can help read the map and navigate through unfamiliar terrain, while younger ones will enjoy the time spent together in sharing stories and playing games. Road trips can be tailored to suit everyone's tastes and stamina – a short trip along the Fairy-Tale Road in Germany, for example, or a longer one up California's coast – and made fun by hiring a vintage car for short trips or a roomier model for cross-country adventures. This is a perfect chance to really get to know a new country, and the view when you get to your final destination (overleaf) makes everything worthwhile.

Travelling by car means that you won't miss the weird and wonderful things that line the roadside and make each destination so interesting and rewarding. A wagon wheel near Sedona in Yavapai County, Arizona suggests visions of the Wild West, while a covered bridge and rich autumn foliage are typical highway scenes in Vermont. Opposite: A lingering remnant of frontier days at Sedona, near the Grand Canyon.

MUSIC TO DRIVE BY There is nothing more stultifying than spending hours on vast stretches of desert or single-lane highways with nothing to look at or inspire, so make the most of the adventure by putting on some music that gets the family excited about where you're going to • Tuning in to local radio stations is a fun way to track how accents and news topics change with the scenery • When driving through the Western states, a rousing chorus of *Home on the Range* or *The Yellow Rose of Texas* is sure to get everyone in the mood • If your trip takes you to the Tuscan countryside, a Pavarotti aria in between stopping off for cups of espresso is the natural choice • When approaching Paris, what could be more appropriate than Edith Piaf singing *La Vie en Rose?* • In Rajasthan, or anywhere else in India for that matter, children will love doing the dance routines in the back seat along to a Bollywood soundtrack • Showtunes or a spirited rendition of *I Want to be in America* from West Side Story is a must for a trip to New York City • Similarly, sea shanties by The Clancy Brothers work for Ireland, as do songs from the Motown era when travelling to the Motor City – Detroit.

sea

Enjoying the water, whether on land or out to sea

Holidays on the water are looked forward to with gleeful anticipation and nervous excitement in equal measure. Part of growing up is learning how to control and enjoy this most elemental of forces, while at the same time respecting its power. It has been recognized that children who are introduced early to swimming and playing in the water grow into kids who are naturally more confident and at ease in the outdoors. There is no end to the water-themed activities that families can enjoy together, from taking a boat out at dawn for a spot of deep-sea fishing to investigating the little creatures who make their homes in tidal pools. Make being on the water an adventure to remember.

A family enjoys time together on the beach during a holiday in North Devon. Here, the rocks along the coast of Rockham Bay are testament to the many historic shipwrecks lying beneath the ocean's surface. The nearby town of Mortehoe dates back to the Domesday Book, and was the former haunt of smugglers and shipwreckers, although today's visitor is more likely to meet surfers and fellow holiday-makers. Overleaf: Surfing at Rockham Bay.

surfing   There are some experiences that children will never forget, and a holiday spent surfing the ocean swells will doubtless be one of them. Children will love trying out a sport that is so associated with a carefree Californian lifestyle, and being free to be cool like the big kids. If you and your children are rank beginners, head for a destination that has a surf school for kids nearby. Their natural balance and innate daredevilry will stand them in good stead as they learn to master the skill – their equally natural impatience, however, may let them down, as surfing is all about waiting patiently for the next big wave. Once mastered, surfing is an activity that everyone in the family can dive into.

WHERE TO GO The big waves around the North Shore of **Oahu** and the other Hawaiian islands attract more experienced surfers, but the conditions make this one of the world's top surfing destinations • Another challenging surfing spot is San Francisco Bay, in **California**, with its stunning views of the city skyline, Golden Gate Bridge and Alcatraz Island (beginners should head to the gentler waters of Southern California) • The Silver Coast, a stretch of land along **France**'s west coast, boasts some of the best swells in Europe – and some of the most glamorous day-trippers and high-rollers in the glamorous city of Biarritz • The beaches along **Australia**'s Sunshine Coast offer top surfing, along with plenty of less arduous activities on the water, including fishing, canoeing and swimming • The popular beach resort of Famara Beach, in the Canary Islands' **Lanzarote**, has also become something of a surfing mecca; a surf school is located at Playa de Famara • And off the southwestern tip of England, the daunting surf of **Cornwall** attracts serious surfers; beginners may find England's eastern coast around Pentewan Beach and Whitsand Bay more suitable.

Fifteen men of 'em good and true

Yo ho ho and a bottle of rum!

Ev'ry man jack could ha' sailed with Old Pew,

Yo ho ho and a bottle of rum!

There was chest on chest of Spanish gold

With a ton of plate in the middle hold

And the cabins riot of stuff untold,

And they lay there that took the plum

With sightless glare and their lips struck dumb

While we shared all by the rule of thumb,

Yo ho ho and a bottle of rum!

From a 1901 musical inspired by ROBERT LOUIS STEVENSON's *Treasure Island*

FAMOUS PIRATES Back in 1881, **Long John Silver** set the pirate standard in *Treasure Island* – wooden legs and parrots are now de rigueur • **Captain Jack Sparrow** in *Pirates of the Caribbean* may be a recent addition to the pirate hall of fame, but is no less engaging for that with children • The notorious real-life pirate **Blackbeard** ravaged the Caribbean seas in the 18th century • Brandishing his hook for a hand, **Captain Hook** in *Peter Pan* introduced us to the terrors of walking the plank • In Gilbert and Sullivan's comic opera *The Pirates of Penzance*, the **Pirate King** and his inept crew did their work off England's south coast • The best-known of history's female pirates is **Anne Bonny**, who eloped with 'Calico Jack' Rackham and joined his crew in the Bahamas • A privateer during the War of the Grand Alliance (1688–97), **Captain William Kidd**'s pirate ships patrolled the eastern seaboard of the New World.

SWIM

Splashing, swirling and floating are wondrous sensations for children, and holidays are the perfect time to dive right in. Some children will relish the feeling of plunging straight into the sea, while others will need coaxing to get into the smallest of pools. If they currently use floats, encourage them to do without; if they can swim a length, challenge them to do five. Agree a reward for meeting their goals by the end of the holiday. Not only will your children learn, but they will find the whole process that bit more exciting.

DIVE

Swimming alongside graceful creatures in a magical land under the sea is a thrilling adventure for any child. Kids' clubs often offer watersports as an inclusive activity, so attempt a little further each day until children feel confident to venture deeper under water. The Great Barrier Reef is at the top of most people's wish lists when it comes to snorkelling, but global warming is a real and present danger for this natural wonder. We can all help our planet by keeping once-in-a-lifetime adventures to just that.

splash

SAIL

Sailing offers a flexible itinerary and the chance to soak up the sea air and changing scenery, and to hop on and off to browse the local markets, meet artisans, or have a clambake on the beach. Whether on a yacht or a wooden boat, a cruise ship or a barge, travelling on the water is a wonderful way for the family to bond. Let children have a go at being Captain and manning the wheel! Many seaside hotels and resorts offer sailing as part of the package, so make the most of it and get out on the water as often as you can.

WATERSKI

Waterskiing is a tough activity for any child to master, and if yours is among those not immediately able to spring up on their skis, getting dragged along behind a boat can be a frightening experience. But like surfing, the feeling of achievement when they do master it is immeasurable. For beginners, let them have a go on a quiet lake, if at all possible – a crowded delta with lots of boats about is probably best avoided. Children who are new to waterskiing may find it comforting to have an adult with them in the water.

DOLPHINS

Along with snorkelling at the Great Barrier Reef, swimming with dolphins also feature highly on people's must-do lists. These enchanting creatures are clearly better off in their natural environment, rather than in a theme park, so ideally join a tour that goes out into the ocean. Most companies only take out small groups, and will offer a refund if you do not get an encounter or sighting. If you are staying at a beach resort, it may well be that dolphin-watching is part of their package or that the hotel can arrange an excursion.

The hardest thing for any parent is to LET GO, and even harder when we're on holiday and miles from **home**. We all think we remember how *freely* we spent our own childhoods, but was it really safer, or is ignorance B L I S S ? Overprotective parents can lead to children who are unable to cope alone. The greatest *gift* we can give our children is to trust a little more and worry a little less.

trust
confidence to let go

fishing When planning holidays near the water, it is worth remembering that occasionally splashing out for a luxury hotel makes sense. Activities such as boating or deep-sea fishing excursions are usually included in the overall price, giving the whole family the opportunity to try out a new kind of adventure and the freedom to repeat the experience every day until children feel more confident. Such holidays are a wonderful chance to introduce children to a new pastime that may very well develop into a lifelong passion – one to cultivate and encourage when you return home.

A father and his sons set off on a fishing adventure from Le Saint Géran resort, in Mauritius. Guests (up to three) can book the Chico II for deep-sea fishing expeditions for a full or half day. Rods and reels are supplied. Local species of fish include black marlin, the larger Atlantic blue marlin, sailfish, yellowfin tuna and wahoo. Pages 138–141: Enjoying the spectacular natural rock pools at Mowani Mountain Camp, in Namibia.

From the moment we are born, and even before, water is *crucial* to our lives. CONTACT with water starts early – from a first bath in the sink to swimming lessons at the local pool. We can all remember the feeling of frantically holding on to the side, and then – finally – the LIBERATING sensation of letting go. Our bodies are *seventy per cent* water, and we all know the necessity of drinking eight glasses a day. Water plays such an important role in our lives, in how much we need it and how much we use it – our very lives DEPEND on it.

water
elemental life force

beyond

Adventures beyond the norm, taking you into the wild

Our greatest adventures happen when we remove ourselves from the everyday to connect to something bigger, bolder, braver. Holidays that challenge our senses and take us to experiences and places that are truly new allow us to do just that, and to feel that we've truly grown and become richer human beings. From the sand dunes of an endless desert to a snow-capped mountain top, the vastness of these surroundings inspires reflection and restores us to a quieter centre in our soul. These big adventures take time to plan and even longer in the anticipation, but the reality still manages to outdo our expectations.

A mother and daughter watch the sun set over Mowani Mountain Camp. Each evening, guests take their places on the rocks and are served chilled drinks and canapés as the sun sets over the African bush. Other activities to enjoy at Mowani (the resort's name comes from the word 'm'wane', meaning 'place of God') are excursions by jeep in search of desert elephants, or a visit to the nearby archaeological site of Twyfelfontein.

safari The origin of the word 'safari' stems from the Arabic term *safariya*, meaning 'to travel', and it hardly needs saying that going on safari is the original adventure. With even the most far-flung destinations now so accessible, safaris can still provide the thrill of a lifetime, and the opportunity to see wild animals in their native habitats. Children's natural curiosity and affinity with animals (a lion's roar and an elephant's bellow are among the first sounds in a child's repertoire) keep them content to wait and see what appears – a precious exercise in patience in a world of instant gratification.

A guestroom at Onguma Tented Camp, located on the edge of Namibia's Etosha National Park, promises nights spent in relaxed luxury. The fabric walls can be rolled away for views of the watering hole, 60 metres away.

Onguma Safari Camp in Namibia offers several accommodation options on the site. Twenty thousand hectares of land support all manner of wild animals – including lions, zebras and giraffes – to be seen from the safety of the jeep and under the watchful eye of the local guide. Here, as on the previous pages, the Tented Camp's luxurious pavilions bespeak a more grown-up holiday. This is a destination for older children (12 and over only)

– and parents must sign a disclaimer that absolves the resort from responsibility if they or their children are eaten up by the local wildlife! For younger children, Onguma Bush Camp is just as inviting – and even provides picnic lunches for the whole family to take on safari. Families who want to get even closer to nature – and have brought their own equipment – can set up camp in the grounds.

The stars awaken a certain reverence,

because though always present, they are inaccessible;

but all natural objects make a kindred impression,

when the mind is open to their influence.

Nature never wears a mean appearance.

Neither does the wisest man extort her secret,

and lose his curiosity by finding out all her perfection.

Nature never became a toy to a wise spirit.

The flowers, the animals, the mountains,

reflected the wisdom of his best hour,

as much as they had delighted

the simplicity of his childhood.

RALPH WALDO EMERSON

At Mowani Mountain Camp, guests can stay in one of twelve luxury tents (top) – each of which has its own wooden deck and en suite – or enjoy the services of a dedicated butler at one of the thatch-covered suites (above, left). A thatched roof of a different kind covers the seating area at The Desert Homestead and Horsetrails, in Namibia (above, right). Opposite: Guesthouses in the evening sun at The Desert Homestead. The Nubib, Tsaris and Naukluft mountains are all within view of the resort, as is the Namib Desert. Overleaf: A moment of repose at Onguma Bush Camp, watched over by a porcine friend.

Think about what is age appropriate. Some camps only take children over the age of 12, but if yours are younger, try to find a camp that will welcome them, too. Even very young children will delight in taking part in the many camp activities.

If your main aim is to see the 'Big Five' (lions, elephants, leopards, rhinos and African buffalo), however, go during the hot, dry season, when the grass is short and visibility good. Be prepared that in other seasons, when rainfall is high, you might not see very much.

Check with the tour operator, and don't be afraid to ask for their record on environmental issues.

Do try to stay at a small, tented camp, as the experience of interacting with the local children and staff is as much a part of the experience as seeing the animals.

Plan to visit a few locations, as the animals you see may be vastly different from one place to the next, and the driving adds to the adventure.

Sunrise and sunset are the best times for safaris, so take a check on your child's body clock. Some camps have nannies that can look after the children while you enjoy the morning excursions; the children join you later on.

Consider combining safaris with a trip to the nearest big city.

For an entirely different kind of adventure, try those that feature bird-watching or venturing out on camels.

'Our task must be to *free* ourselves
by widening our circle of compassion
to embrace all living creatures and the
whole of nature and its *beauty*.'

ALBERT EINSTEIN

wild

circle of life

Tales of gods and heroes, good and *evil* are an important part of our cultural identity, and children all over the world love to hear them *told* or read aloud. Stories that come from a time when people relied on the land were a means of sharing and passing on knowledge. Today, they are just as *enthralling* for little ears.

legend sharing stories

sand dunes An awfully big adventure for any child – sand dunes allow us all to be intrepid explorers with no fear of boundaries. We can scramble up or slide down their sugary slopes, knowing the sand will cushion us when we fall. When seeing our children in these unrestrained surroundings, it is hard not to wince at the hours spent in front of the television. Give them the chance to run free and you will discover that what they really want is to find their own way, knowing you are close at hand.

This little explorer hits the Sossusvlei Sand Dunes, in Namibia's Namib-Naukluft Park, picking up creepy-crawlies and discovering the little creatures behind the footprints. The nearby resort of Wolwedans, located in the NamibRand Nature Reserve, provides a luxurious base from which to explore the unspoilt dunes. In keeping with their ecological ethos, the resort makes sure there are 1,000 hectares of nature for every bed at Wolwedans.

WHERE TO FIND THEM The highest in Namibia, the **Sossusvlei** sand dunes are also among the world's tallest • The best way to see the **Jaisalmer** sand dunes in India is by camel, stopping off to watch some Rajasthani folk dancing to traditional music as the sun sets • Both red and white sand dunes can be found in this region of Vietnam: white dunes at **Bao Trang**, and red dunes a bit further south at **Muí Ne** • Stay at the Hotel Yasmina Merzouga for access to the **Erg Chebbi** dunes in Morocco; the hotel's lake is the place to spot flamingos • Located at Cape Reinga in New Zealand, where the Tasman Sea and the Pacific Ocean meet, the **Te Paki** sand dunes are the tallest in the country; the famous 145-kilometre beach is nearby • The white sand dunes of **New Mexico** are a national monument located in the Tularosa Basin, near Alamogordo • Stunning dunes set against the rocky ridges of the Sangre de Cristo Mountains can be found at the Grand Sand Dunes National Park of **Colorado** • The red **Wahiba** dunes in the Ash-Sharqiyah region of Oman are still inhabited by Bedouin tribes; a tourist camp is 13 kilometres from the dunes, and guided tours run out of Muscat.

Natural wonders leave us with a profound feeling of PEACE, one that we can carry home with us in our hearts. The hope is that we return changed for the experience, with a desire to give something back to the Earth for the protection it provides – even if that means making small but simple changes in the way we live at home. If we care for our planet, it gives us so much more in return.

horizon no limits

skiing A world away from the heat of the African sun, ski resorts provide a playground for all ages. Whether you want to master the form or just indulge in the views, there is something elemental and restorative about being surrounded by pure white snow. Alpine resorts will more often than not offer lessons to beginners, and the sooner children get started, the better to foster both skill and a lasting love of the outdoors. Unlike contact sports, skiing allows children to improve and grow in confidence at their own pace, with the ultimate goal of conquering the bunny slopes and just having fun.

Children throwing themselves into the moment and snowballs at each other at this ski resort in Italy. The five-star Kempinski Pragelato Village is a chalet complex with luxurious service, together with direct access to the slopes via cable car.

The flickering flame of the *northern lights* could be plainly seen, whether they rose high or low in the *HEAVENS*, from every part of the castle. In the midst of its empty, endless hall of *snow* was a frozen lake, broken on its surface into a thousand forms; each piece resembled another, from being in itself PERFECT as a work of art, and in the centre of this lake sat the *Snow Queen*.

HANS CHRISTIAN ANDERSEN, *The Snow Queen*

CROSS-COUNTRY

For children who are hesitant at first about downhill skiing, try introducing them to the cross-country variety, which can be a bit gentler on bumped knees. If you and your family are new to the sport, you might consider going in the off-season or mid-week. Even the most adventurous of children may not take to skiing immediately, and it is not uncommon for the first few days of ski lessons to end in tears. Be sure not to rush your child; as with anything, skiing – whether cross-country or downhill – just needs a bit of time and practice.

SLED

Playing outside in the snow is one of the true joys of childhood. Make sure your intrepid snowmen-builders dress snugly in lots of layers; ski gear has become fashionable for kids, and it is tempting to succumb to their demands for style over substance. Keeping warm is the key to getting the most out of time spent outdoors, and if children feel cold or uncomfortable they will be less likely to try something new. Keep a thermos of hot chocolate handy, along with a little dried fruit for when energy starts to sag.

snow

SLEIGH RIDE

What winter adventure is complete without a sleigh ride to the tune of jangling bells, pulled by a pair of shaggy ponies or a team of huskies? Or, should your travels take you to Lapland, by a reindeer? Sleighs have become firmly associated in our imaginations with the festive season, and a ride in one while bundled up in extra jumpers and woolly hats is as eagerly anticipated as a visit to Santa. Almost any snowy region will offer their own version of a sleigh ride, all guaranteed to make passengers feel merry and bright.

FUN IN THE SNOW

How lucky if you are able to rush outside at the first real snowfall and make snow angels to your heart's content. But for those who live in milder climes, there is plenty of fun to be had on even a short visit to the snow. Apart from the ever-popular snowball fight (although do ensure that children throw snowballs gently – when thrown with force, they hurt), some other games to enjoy are tug-of-war, with everyone digging their snowboots into the soft powder, and seeing who can toss a hat onto the top of a snowman.

SKI

Skiing holidays are a wonderful option for families with especially sporty or active children. Look for resorts that have plenty of bunny slopes and dedicated children's areas, and for those that match your child's skiing ability (resorts that feature black runs, for example, probably aren't suitable), rather than your desire to hobnob with the rich and famous. Book well in advance as good resorts tend to fill up early. And if they are not included, don't forget to factor in ski lessons as part of the holiday budget.

trekking   Holidays involving trekking and hiking are best for families with either babies, who can be carried on backs, or children old enough to stand the pace (7 and up). It is probably best to save higher altitudes for a return trip, as children may not take to it and it's a little late once you are up there. Depending on where you want to go and how long you decide to go for, treks can range from simple, such as a pony ride to the bottom of a canyon, to strenuous – although if you choose the latter, make sure you choose a location where support is readily available. You might also consider joining a group or teaming up with friends, so that there are plenty of people around and places to see and stop at along the way to heighten the spirit of adventure for children.

The Rohtang Pass in Himachal Pradesh connects the Kullu, Lahul and Spiti valleys in the Indian Himalayas. Before heading up the pass, this family hired their fur coats from one of the many roadside mountain-clothing emporiums, and a sherpa to help them ascend above the snow line. The tents and sleeping bags were obtained through local guides, and the expedition's cook made sure that no one went hungry. Making use of local knowledge is surely the best way of getting the most out of adventures such as this on a grand scale.

WHERE TO GO It's not just about Mt Everest anymore – trekking through the villages and lower slopes of the **Himalayas** can be a life-changing experience • Don't miss the Lao Cai to Tavanh trail in **Vietnam**, but beware – the tropical climes can occasionally be overwhelming, so make sure kids drink plenty of water • Trek with camels across the sand dunes of **Morocco**, or on mules to the Berber villages in the Atlas Mountains • Hike across the Julian Alps in **Slovenia**'s Triglav National Park for fantastic views of Mt Triglav, the alps' highest peak • When in Australia, head to Wentworth Falls and the Greater Blue Mountains World Heritage Area in New South Wales • Located in the Fiordland National Park of **New Zealand**, the walk at Milford Sound covers 55 kilometres over six days • Follow a camel trek to the **Sinai** with a diving holiday in the Red Sea • Experience the Wild West with a trekking adventure into the Rockies of **Colorado**.

escape

There will be those times when we want to get away from it all and crave a little indulgence, and need a holiday that allows us to escape out of the everyday and into our dreams. Everyone needs a break now and then that revives tired spirits and is just that little bit special, doing whatever it is that pleases, with no demands and not having to work too hard at anything. For some, the perfect embodiment of such a holiday might be a relaxing massage within sight and sound of waves gently lapping on the shore, or catching up on some long overdue reading by a log fire. For others, it might be playing a leisurely game of golf on a world-famous course, or simply enjoying the company of family and friends in a rented house in the country. Children will have their own ideas of what constitutes the perfect break, and might prefer the thrill of a theme park, exploring a real-life fairy-tale castle, or taking part in activities at a beach resort's kids' club. Whatever the choice, this chapter is all about a little escapism and a lot of unadulterated fun.

resort

Taking time out for a little holiday indulgence

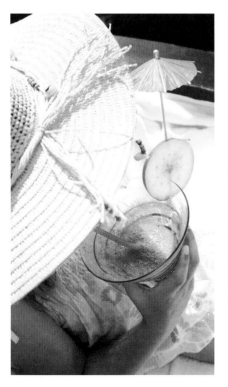

Staying at a beach resort is all about stepping into an alternative world, one in which our every desire is anticipated and provided for. It might seem terribly extravagant, but it is bliss to luxuriate once in a while in a bath strewn with rose petals, or to sleep between cool, scented sheets that have been changed daily by unseen hands, and to leave your room in the morning knowing that everything will have magically cleaned itself by the time you return. Kids' clubs are also an increasingly prominent fixture at many resorts. They may seem like marketing hype, but how much nicer it is for parents to enjoy their holiday when safe in the knowledge that the kids are entertained and cared for.

It's not what you do, but how you do it: a holiday-maker enjoys a cool drink – with the all-important umbrella – and a little afternoon reading by the pool. Previous pages: Blossoms of frangipani, the local flower of Mauritius, form a pretty necklace that's easy for children to create on their own. Pages 172–173: A tropical sunset over a clear, blue sea – here at the Taj Exotica Resort &Spa – instantly transports us from the cares of our busy modern lives.

time to be Children need a rest from their hurried lives, and being shuttled from one after-school activity to the next. Teaching them to stop and just be is a true gift; without this ability, children (and, indeed, all of us) run the risk of becoming frenzied and unfocused. Our dearest wish is that our children's lives will be easier, with less pressure than ours, but since we cannot control the future, the best we can do is to instil in our children the awareness that moments taken to stop and savour the world around us are to be treasured.

It would be hard to imagine a more perfect setting for a luxurious holiday than here at the Taj Exotica Resort & Spa, in Mauritius. Overleaf: Young guests enjoy seeing what the grown-ups get up to, in this case, enjoying an old-fashioned cabaret, while a dancer practises her routine as she waits to go on stage at Le Saint Géran hotel.

MAKING THE MOST OF YOUR STAY Does the hotel offer courtesy transport to and from the airport? • Are you being given a room with a view? • Does the hotel include excursions and all recreational activities, including the kids' club, within its price? • Check the hotel's policy on baby-sitting and listening devices • Ask for rooms away from public areas, as they can go on for all hours and interrupt children's sleep, as well as your own evening enjoyment • Let the hotel know in advance of any requirements relating to allergies • Ask the hotel to email you a timetable of events so that you can plan for particular activities • Be careful about asking hotel staff for recommendations as they may suggest places because of a personal interest rather than on merit • If you want the mini-bar emptied, just ask that it be done and restock the refrigerator with your own essentials • Leave the laptop behind, but if you must work, take a flash card instead • When handing in laundry, be sure to provide any special instructions for washing • While you will want to leave tips for good service to various members of staff, your personal concierge should get the biggest tip, to be given on departure.

What does it mean to **indulge**, to let go and treat our bodies with *kindness*? After having children, we can become so FOCUSED on their needs that sometimes our own get lost, a state that benefits no one. When we spend our days looking after others, allowing someone else to take CARE of us is a **treat** to be savoured – and not having to worry about time and responsibilities is a wonderful thing.

indulge relax and renew

alternative therapies The benefits of healing with hands and homeopathic remedies have never been mysterious to many cultures around the world, and now we, too, have woken up to the fact that such therapies can play an important part in our lives, and to the essential value of harmony and balance to health. Luxury resorts and spas increasingly feature these kinds of treatments, and are an ideal place in which to experiment and discover what works for you.

At the Taj Exotica Spa & Resort in Mauritius, ayurvedic healing is the order of the day. Ayurveda has its roots in the Indian subcontinent, and is based on the principle that good health is achieved and maintained when the three bodily humours, or doshas, are in balance. The resort has an ayurvedic doctor on call, and offers treatments in two rooms devoted to the practice.

This is your time.

Take some time to look around the spa
before booking treatments, and ask all
the questions you need to.

Check the spa's cancellation policy and
give plenty of notice for any changes.

Arrive a good 20 minutes early to give
yourself time to check in, get changed
and complete forms, and even earlier
if you intend to make use of the spa's
other facilities, such as the steam
room and pool.

Ideally, do not eat or drink too much
prior to your treatment.

Wear loose, comfortable clothing,
and if you don't want to get fully
undressed – don't.

Your therapist will want you to enjoy
your treatment, and to be told if you
would like changes in room temperature,
music, lighting, or if she is applying too
much or too little pressure. And if you
want to sleep, just do so.

Leave the phone and all thoughts behind.
To do the treatment justice, allow
yourself the time to enjoy it fully.

Check if the gratuity is included. If not,
leave between 10 to 20 per cent,
depending on your level of satisfaction.

EPACHA GAME LODGE & SPA, NAMIBIA

This retreat, Namibia's first five-star lodge, is set in a private game reserve bordering the Etosha National Park, and offers private chalets, each of which has its own patio and outdoor shower with views across the African bush. A relaxing array of treatments is also on offer, ideal for those wanting a little luxe at the end of a day spent on safari. Children can enjoy a mini-manicure, while their parents can indulge in a long soak or a drink at the bar. The hotel also has a private wing for family celebrations, complete with its own butler.

AMANSALA, CANCUN

A mere four-hour flight from New York, the Amansala resort promises adventure. A visit here is, the resort claims, a bit like staying in Robinson Crusoe's beach hut – only a lot more luxurious. The spa features Mayan clay treatments, and outings to the nearby Mayan ruins can be organized, but all agree that the real draw here is the Bikini Boot Camp. Restricted to 25 guests, the boot camp is an intense six-day programme of activity and yoga. The aim is not necessarily weight loss, but rather achieving a more balanced lifestyle and feeling good about yourself. Bliss.

spas

THE GROVE, HERTFORDSHIRE

Located within an 18th-century stately home deep in the English countryside, The Grove is the perfect antidote to city life. The state-of-the-art Sequoia Spa has a cavernous black mosaic-tiled pool, as well as candlelit treatment and relaxation rooms. Several spa packages are available, tailored to golfers (who will appreciate the course designed by Kyle Phillips), couples, or those who just require a bit of extra pampering. There is plenty for the children, too, with dedicated children's menus and special activities for families on half-term break.

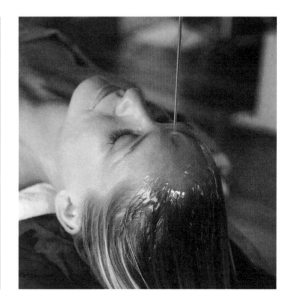

TAJ EXOTICA RESORT & SPA, MAURITIUS

This French Colonial-inspired resort is the last word in romance, boasting private villas with ocean views, a pool and an outdoor lounging area. There are two restaurants at the resort, along with a stylish outdoor bar, or guests may choose to dine elsewhere on the island. The superb kids' club will keep children occupied while their mums participate in the yoga and meditation classes, followed by the spa's signature two-hour massage or a visit to the ayurvedic spa. Deep-sea fishing, island exploration and seaplane excursions are also available.

PARROT CAY, TURKS & CAICOS ISLANDS

This beautiful 1,000-acre resort is housed on its own private island. The COMO Shambhala sanctuary is located here, an holistic spa that aims to treat mind, body and spirit together. An ayurvedic doctor is on call, and yoga fans can take advantage of the five-day Yoga Shanti retreat. Pilates classes and boat trips are some of the other leisurely ways of spending time at this luxurious resort. As for food, Parrot Cay naturally emphasizes raw ingredients, and menus feature plenty of fresh fruit and seafood. Opposite: A treatment room at the Taj Exotica Resort & Spa.

PIZZA DOUGH

1 cup warm water
1 packet active dry yeast
2½ to 3 cups all-purpose flour
2 tablespoons olive oil
½ teaspoon salt

Combine the water, yeast and half of the flour in a large bowl. Add the oil, salt and remaining flour, and mix well. Place the dough on a floured surface and knead until smooth. Transfer the dough to a lightly oiled bowl. Cover the bowl with a tea towel, and let the dough rest. When the dough has doubled in size, place it on a floured surface, divide into two parts, and roll them into balls. Cover them with a towel and let rest for 15 minutes. Then shape, cover with favourite toppings, and cook. Then eat!

activities Dedicated kids' clubs at hotels and resorts are a relatively recent innovation, but children and parents both have been quick to embrace them. Such is the popularity of the clubs that the facilities often rival those catering to more grown-up guests. Children from toddlers to teens can dip in and out throughout the day, meeting and sharing meals with new friends and trying out activities that might otherwise not be available to them. They will want to be at the kids' club rather than anywhere else.

Here at the KidsOnly club at Le Saint Géran, Mauritius, a would-be chef gets to grips with the fine art of stone-baked pizza. Supervision is always close to hand, and parents can feel perfectly safe in leaving their children free to enjoy the many activities on offer.

Children are in tune to their own kind of fun and way of
escaping into their *imaginations*, and leaving them free once
in a while to choose how they spend their time makes for
a happy child and a happier holiday all round. It's all about
creating experiences to enrich and remember – sometimes
these are best discovered on your own.

free

discovering the world

ÉVIAN ROYAL RESORT, FRANCE

Évian Royal Resort, set within 45 acres of parkland, is a place that was created with children in mind. There are two options for young guests: the Kids' Resort caters to children aged two to 11, while the Royal Rider is for 12- to 16-year-olds. On the roster of activities are sculpting, archery, and even a mini-Olympics. Water sports, including waterskiing, are to be had on nearby Lake Geneva, at the foot of the French Alps. Golf lessons, mountain hikes and snow-shoe treks are also available, all in keeping with the hotel's aim of pushing your limits.

THE ICKWORTH HOTEL, SUFFOLK

This 18th-century stately home, once the seat of the aristocratic Hervey family, is now the site of a luxury family hotel, deep in the English countryside. The East Wing of the house is given over exclusively to families, with the Four Bears' Den keeping young children happily occupied throughout the day, after which tea is served at 5. Teens and older children can enjoy table tennis, games and videos at Club/Blu. Outside, the list of activities continues: swimming, bike riding, hiking along the nature trails in the grounds, and enjoying the hotel's 'adventure playground'.

kids' clubs

SEA ISLAND RESORT, GEORGIA

The recipient of *Golf Digest*'s award for Best Golf Course in North America (2006), this resort on an island off the US state of Georgia opened in 1928 and is still owned by the same family. The Camp Cloisters kids' club divides activities into age groups, with older children participating in overnight camp-outs, kayaking, horseback riding, teen makeovers and a visit to a wildlife refuge. There are plenty of activities for the younger children, too, including visits to the on-site ice-cream parlour. The annual Fourth of July parade is also a much-anticipated event.

LE SAINT GÉRAN, MAURITIUS

Le Saint Géran is is well known for its beautiful white beaches and six-star hotel, which offers blissful relaxation at its spa and gourmet indulgence at its Alain Ducasse-backed restaurant, Spoon des Îles. Kids will also enjoy their stay here, taking part in the many activities organized by the KidsOnly club, for children aged four to 11. The clubhouse has a swimming pool, play areas, computer stations, and even its own restaurant. Teens are not left out, as the resort offers activities for 12- to 17-year-olds, such as day trips, disco dances and themed evenings.

FRÉGATE ISLAND, SEYCHELLES

Frégate Island, the easternmost island of the Seychelles, boasts a luxury holiday resort in addition to its rich bird- and plantlife. A full-service spa is on hand for frazzled mums, but the big draw is the Castaway Club, exclusively for children between the ages of five and 12. In addition to offering the usual games and crafts, the resort also is keen to raise environmental awareness among even its youngest guests. A special clubhouse offers classes and activities to educate youngsters about the ecology and conservation of the island's heritage. Opposite: The maze at Sea Island.

ocean What is it about the beach that lets our minds go? The ocean of our imagination is a pure, boundless sea, one that gives us a feeling of serenity and peace. We return to the beach throughout our lives, to recall and reconnect with childhood memories. The smells and sounds of the sea takes us back to a time when we ran free, knowing that the sand would protect us from any fall and that we had all day to spend engrossed in digging, collecting pebbles and seashells, inventing games and building the perfect sandcastle (see overleaf). Life as adults may be rather more involved, but a day at the beach, with its views disappearing over the horizon, reminds us of the bigger picture.

GAMES IN THE SAND Going crabbing and investigating tide pools for sea urchins and anemones • Beach volleyball, a perennial favourite • Sand angels • Embracing your inner acrobat with human pyramids • Games of 'It' and tag in the shallow tide • Making seaweed beards and skipping ropes out of giant strands of kelp • Playing kick-the-bucket, once you have tipped out the contents to make your sandcastle. Above: A walk along the beach in Mauritius, hand-in-hand, at the end of a long day of fun and games. Opposite: Footprints in the sand and a necklace of frangipani, with the resort of Le Saint Géran and the setting sun in the distance.

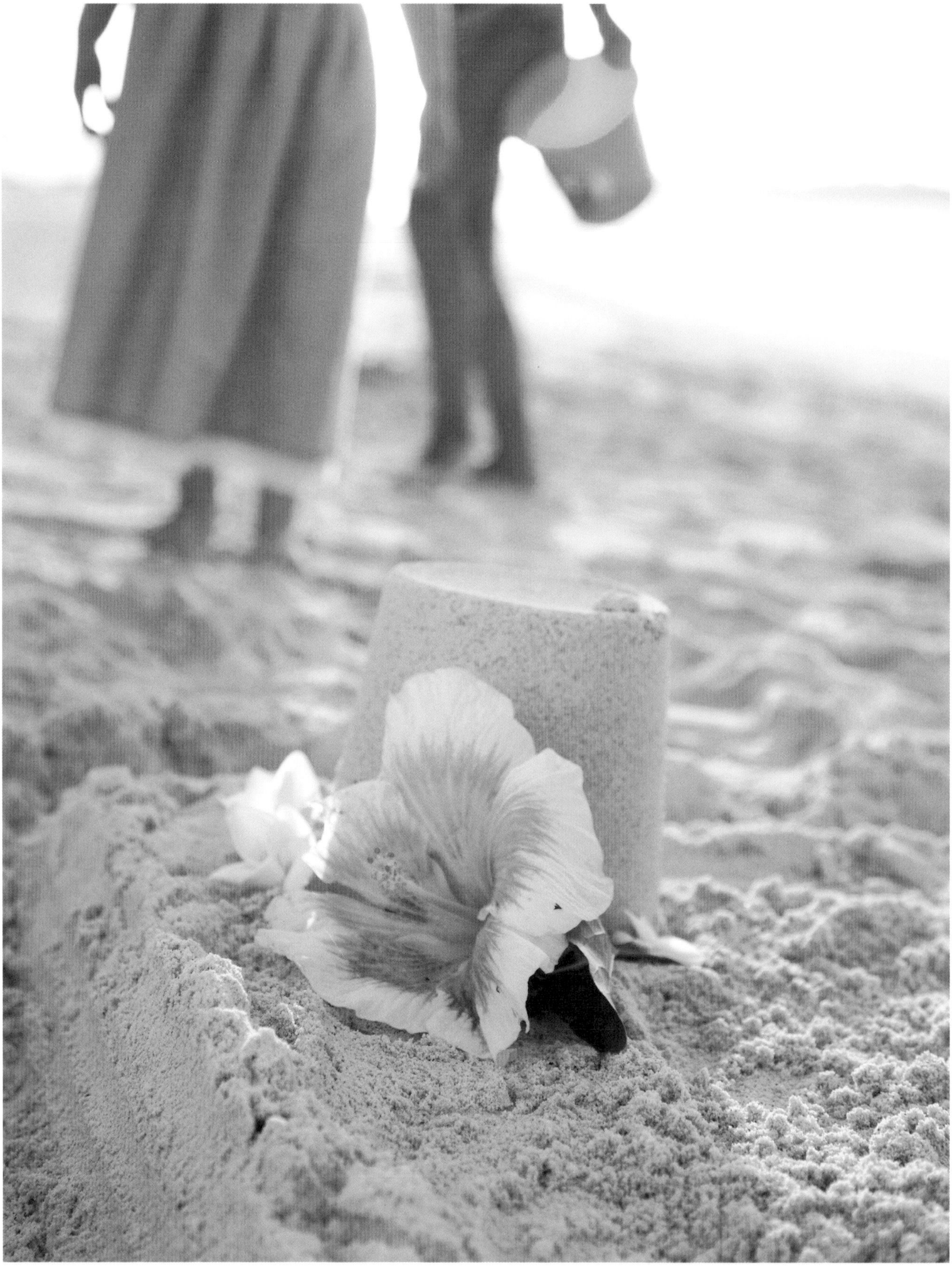

According to recent research by Bournemouth University, one part water to eight parts sand is the ideal ratio for a perfect sandcastle. It is best to build your castle close to the water, forming sand patties the size and shape of a thick pancake. Once the tower is built, gently carve it into shape using a small plastic shovel or spatula, and then smooth over the castle with wet sand for a perfect finish. Overleaf: A colourful array of deckchairs on a beach in Sitges, near Barcelona, await the first sun-seekers of the day.

There were other trees in the garden, and one of the things which made the place look strangest and *loveliest* was that climbing roses had run all over them and swung down long tendrils which made light swaying curtains, and here and there they had caught at each other or at a far-reaching branch and had crept from one TREE to another and made lovely bridges of themselves.

FRANCES HODGSON BURNETT, *The Secret Garden*

flower colour and beauty

imagine

Setting your inner fairy-tale princess free

An imaginative and inquisitive mind is a wonderful thing in any child, and family holidays provide the ideal environment for encouraging curiosity about the countries you visit together and about the world we live in today. You may feel that the castles of Ireland and the châteaux of France are too far away for a holiday, but the history of places closer to home are ripe for exploration, too, and offer every bit as much in the way of a rewarding day out. Living villages, ghost towns, historic railroads and mazes — all of these places offer much in the way of engaging children's interest in the people that lived and worked there before, and consequently in their own surroundings.

Visiting a castle, or even staying in one, is a magical experience, whatever your age. Opposite: A young guest at Dromoland Castle, in Ireland's Co. Clare, is all dressed up with somewhere important to go. Dromoland Castle is located in the western part of the country, near the popular destinations of Limerick and Galway and with views of the Shannon River and the rocky Burren landscape, home to a treasure trove of archaeological sites.

make believe Fairy-tales play an important part in the early development of a child's curiosity and imagination, and children are naturally drawn to fantastical legends of derring-do. Visiting a real-life castle (or a palace, a stately home, *palazzo* or grand villa) gives children the opportunity to play a leading role in their very own story – whether a princess in a tower or a gallant knight to rescue her. History comes alive in a more immediate way when the towers and dungeons of the past are right there in front of you.

Dromoland Castle offers plenty of scope for young imaginations to run free. Here, a tea party prepared by the hotel's chef is carefully laid out in the castle's turret. The turret was erected by the 2nd Baronet Inchiquin, who had gambled his estate on a horse race, in gratitude to his winning horse, Sean Buis. The horse's resting place can be seen in the temple at the bottom of the garden.

staying in a castle Visiting an ancient castle is a special thrill for children, particularly those who love the stories of history, but staying in one is even better. Hotel rooms and corridors take on an extra layer of allure when the furniture is Jacobean and intricately carved, and a suit of armour stands guard outside your room. Family portraits, stained glass and imposing vaulting all add to the feeling that you are staying somewhere very special, indeed. Parents are happy when holidays are enhanced with a sprinkling of education, and children are having too much fun to notice a little learning thrown in.

Dromoland Castle is a glamorous and special place for grown-ups to stay, but the hotel also makes an extra effort on behalf of its younger guests. Children are greeted with a Dromoland teddy bear and with cookies individually decorated with their names. Specially prepared children's menus and board games are also on offer, and castle staff can arrange horseback riding lessons at the nearby stables. Opposite: Children happily adhere to the hotel's policy of encouraging guests to treat the castle as if it was their own.

DROMOLAND CASTLE, IRELAND

Dromoland Castle has a long and distinguished history as the ancestral home of the O'Brien family, Barons of Inchiquin. Regularly voted among the best hotels in Ireland and the UK, Dromoland has plenty in the way of country pursuits for visitors to enjoy, including fishing, clay shooting, golf and archery, as well as a newly renovated spa. Guests are presented with hotel robes and slippers (children receive junior versions), and can even order a picnic, complete with a bottle of Champagne, from the hotel's chef to take into the grounds.

AMBERLEY CASTLE, ENGLAND

This luxury castle tucked away in the South Downs of West Sussex offers much to appeal to visitors wishing to experience a taste of medieval England. The castle itself is over 900 years old in parts, and is entered through an enormous, two-tonne oak portcullis, which is ceremoniously lowered every evening at midnight. A thatched tree house (see below), reached by a rope bridge, will satisfy younger guests, while the tennis court, golf course and spa will no doubt be welcomed by their parents. The entire castle can also be booked for special occasions.

castles

CHÂTEAU RIGAUD, FRANCE

The idea behind this castle hotel is holiday as house party, where guests either rent the entire 14th-century château or spend time with other family groups. Child care is on hand to allow the grown-ups a rest (particularly welcome to single parents), and every evening the children have supper together in the large kitchen. Activities can be arranged to occupy kids during the day, and there is a cinema and fully stocked DVD library. Everything is designed to give parents a relaxing break and children a bit of fun in the French countryside.

TAJ LAKE PALACE, INDIA

What could be more glamorous than this glorious palace, hovering magically on Lake Pichola? The Taj Lake Palace, located in Udaipur provides the ultimate Indian holiday. The lack of a kids' club hardly matters when guests are greeted with a welcome procession of elephants and camels, and are kept entertained by performances of music and dancing, fireworks displays, and puppet shows for the children. Vintage cars are also on hand to ferry guests to and from the airport, and can be booked for sightseeing tours.

TORRE PALAZZONE, ITALY

The staff at this traditional turreted *palazzo* in Tuscany, located only 12 kilometres from Siena, are determined to make your visit both luxurious and worry-free. On call is a concierge who will arrange restaurant and museum bookings, sightseeing excursions, and even wine tours and tastings (Montepulciano is nearby). Child care is available, and even the *palazzo*'s resident labradors are on hand to accompany guests on their walks through the surrounding Tuscan countryside. The entire villa can be rented, and can host house parties of up to 22 guests.

simple pleasures For a dose of culture and history, visits to museums and the great sights certainly have their place, but sometimes a little gentle introduction to how other people live is good, too. Tourist destinations have taken on board that an endless round of tours of stately homes can be fatiguing. Now the grounds of these houses also offer learning experiences, geared to children who will enjoy the day so much more for a bit of time spent outside. Living villages and restored cottages will often have staff dressed in period costume, food on offer that is native to the region, and livestock to visit – and perhaps even to cuddle. Handicrafts, such as woollen goods and glassware, that reflect the traditional industries of the area are often available, or made on site. A country pub or two can usually be found at these destinations as well – a welcome sight for parents after a long day of sightseeing.

Whiling away a summer's day playing games and making daisy chains in the grounds of Bunratty Castle & Folk Park, in Co. Clare, Ireland. Opposite: A game of hopscotch and a bicycle propped against the wall of a local pub are charming reminders of old-fashioned, simpler pleasures. Overleaf: Visitors to the castle will encounter a traveller's caravan and thatched cottages in the Folk Park.

WHERE TO GO Wild Wadi Water Park is located in the Bab Al Shams resort in **Dubai**, between the Jumeirah Beach and Burj Al Arab hotels • Parc Astérix in **Paris** is an unusual concept in theme parks, based on the stories by Albert Uderzo and René Goscinny • In **Copenhagen**, Tivoli Gardens is the world's second-oldest amusement park, complete with wooden roller-coaster • Corn dogs, arcade games and historic rides are the order of the day at Santa Cruz Beach Boardwalk, in **California**, on the edge of the Pacific Ocean • Wurstelprater in **Vienna** features a giant Ferris wheel and late-night opening hours during the season • **Rajasthan** has many villages, including Shilp Gram, that preserve the local way of life • Rye Playland is situated on the edge of Long Island Sound, a handy destination for those staying in **Manhattan** • At Harbour Park in **West Sussex**, an indoor play centre and roller-coaster are new for this year.

carousel Yes, they may fill you with dread, but theme parks are here to stay. Children adore them, and the more excessive, the better: roller-coasters, arcade amusements, hot dogs and candy floss, there is seemingly no end to the tackiness in store. But there will always be time for culture, and indeed most theme parks are located close to a city, so it is easy to combine funfairs with fine art. Even if a day out at a theme park may not be your idea of fun, your children will be delighted if you come out of your comfort zone and get into the spirit of things.

At this funfair in El Puerto de Santa María, in Spain, a little girl means business in the dodgems. In addition to the one seen here in the Cádiz region, Aqualand has seven locations throughout Spain, as well as parks in Portugal and France. Opposite: A merry-go-round horse is put through its paces.

retreat

Places of quiet and repose, to restore the soul

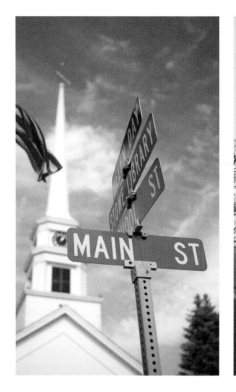

Sometimes a break needs to be just that, a respite and total retreat from the daily toils of looking after house and home. On these occasions, a strenuous holiday involving adventure and activity just won't do, and we long instead to put our feet up at a bed-and-breakfast in a country village over a weekend, or really embrace the concept of time away and spend a month at a Tuscan villa. Each corner of the world has its quiet retreats, with their own rhythms and traditions, and when we visit we have the chance to step into a different life, if only for a few days. Embracing these new activities during our stay, from buying bread at the local shop to paying a visit to the village fête, is all part of the fun of being there.

Tranquillity and peace of mind can be found in all kinds of places, wherever you may choose to travel. Opposite, left to right: A flag flutters in the breeze over a typical Main Street of rural America, in this case Stowe, Vermont; a 12th-century church tower in Norfolk, England provides a focus point for calm reflection; and a bright, sun-washed Spanish street in Vejer de la Frontera offers its own idyllic charms.

sleepy town Holidays in small towns are all about slowing down the pace and finding a rhythm that is a welcome antidote to our hectic, workaday lives. There is ample time to explore and really get to know your temporary home, particularly if your stay is a longer one. Sleepy villages – from Cornwall to Vermont – can be friendly places, where discovering where to do the laundry and take the children to lunch is a pleasant experience rather than an overwhelming one. The bonus for children is that they are easy to navigate, allowing youngsters precious freedom to stretch their wings a little and explore on their own.

In Padstow, a fishing village on the north coast of Cornwall made famous by its hometown celebrity chef and his four restaurants, a bright hat to keep the summer sun at bay and a faithful companion are all that is needed for an afternoon's adventure. Overleaf: Idyllic scenes at Whitstable, in Kent, and on Lake Champlain, in Vermont.

A sense of community is vital to our sense of *wellbeing*. It suggests a place we return to, one that is full of memories and evokes feelings of COMFORT and contentedness, especially now that our lives have become so fragmented. While some things change with the passage of time, some things never do, and the K N O W L E D G E that a street or a tree will be exactly as you remembered never fails to please. *Community* means going home.

autumn home comforts

house Going away to relax need not involve the formality of an
hotel. A simpler, and perhaps more enjoyable, option is to club
together with a group of friends and rent a house in the country,
whether for a weekend, a couple of weeks, or even longer. Getting
together a house party not only shares out the cost, but also allows
the grown-ups time to relax and enjoy themselves without keeping
one eye permanently on the children. And for the children themselves,
there is more fun to be had, as well as safety, in numbers.

*Not all houses available to rent are as grand as this 16th-century one in Norfolk! Opposite: A tray
set with warm scones and hot tea, a comfortable armchair, a long soak and a freshly scrubbed
kitchen table are among a country house's time-honoured pleasures. Previous pages: Holiday-makers
from all over the world travel to New England for its historic towns and to see for themselves the
beauty of its autumn foliage.*

GUESTHOUSE

The renting of guesthouses is big business in India. Hiring one of these large venues is a wonderful chance to gather a big group together and spend time with the generations, with both grandparents and grandchildren on holiday together. Sharing out the cost makes this a less daunting prospect than it might seem; the bigger the group, the better. Popular locations include Mumbai, New Delhi, Bangalore, Hyderabad and Goa. Right: This charming guesthouse in India is a typical example of the kinds of houses on offer.

COUNTRY HOUSE

When renting a country house, whether in the UK or further afield, be sure to book through a tour operator to avoid any unexpected surprises, or go with first-hand recommendations. Check what is included in the way of facilities and additional support, if needed. Houses can include as much or as little as you want in the way of amenities – some even come provided with their own staff! Or you can take the keys and treat the house as your own home away from home. Left and below: At home in Norfolk.

rent

VILLA

Long-term villa rental has become firmly associated with Tuscany, and indeed there are wonderful houses to rent throughout the area. The close proximity to museums, wineries (*enotecas*), and the great cities of the region – Florence and Siena – make Tuscany a perennially attractive proposition. Other destinations are worth exploring, too, such as Catalonia, in Spain, and the hugely popular Provence, in southwestern France. Right: One of the historic slate-covered farmhouses that are seen all over Provence.

CABIN

Abraham Lincoln famously grew up in one, and you, too, can re-create the frontier experience by renting a cabin, log or otherwise, in any one of many rural outposts scattered across the United States. In such a vast and varied country, plenty of different experiences await holiday-makers: in Oregon, you can pan for gold and take a ride on an historic railway during your stay, while in Georgia cabins are available to rent in the beautiful Blue Ridge mountains. Left: A cabin, complete with veranda (convenient for hanging out the washing), in Stowe, Vermont.

COTTAGE

Renting a cottage is a somewhat smaller and less grand, but no less enjoyable, prospect than booking a country house. The National Trust is a good resource for cottages to rent in England, Wales and Northern Ireland (for Scotland, see the National Trust for Scotland), while cottages in Ireland can be found through any number of agencies – Wexford on the south-east coast and Co. Mayo in the west of the country are popular destinations. Right: A thatched cottage in rural Ireland makes for the perfect retreat, as this young traveller has discovered.

peace Days in the country take on their own rhythms, with each member of the family free to indulge in reading, playing games, taking long walks, or just sitting around the kitchen table with a cup of tea. Children never tire of hearing stories of when you were young, and when better to tell them all over again than when you are together and have endless days of freedom stretching before you? The time will come soon enough when holidays like these will become all too few, and the children will no longer be the babes-in-arms they seemed to be five minutes ago. All the more reason to savour our precious holidays, each moment of which is destined to become a cherished memory when we return home.

Strawberries, biscuits and a shelf-ful of old favourites are the perfect accompaniments to a lazy day in this rented house in Norfolk. Exploring the many unfamiliar nooks and crannies of your temporary home is fun, too. Overleaf: In Namibia, the setting sun signals the end of a memorable family holiday.

go

A directory of hotels, spas, castles, museums and more, all of which feature in this book. Numbers in brackets refer to the page numbers on which the destination appears.

HOTELS

Ayasofya Pansiyonlari [45]
A row of nine wooden guesthouses in a quiet, traffic-free street
Sogukcesme Street, Sultanahmet
34400 Istanbul, Turkey
T +90 212 513 3660
E info@ayasofyakonaklari.com
W www.ayasofyapensions.com

Bauer Palladio Hotel & Spa [42]
Five-star boutique hotel with a wellness spa
Giudecca, 33
30133 Venice, Italy
T +39 41 520 7022
E booking@bauervenezia.it
W www.palladiohotelspa.it

The Berkeley [63]
Featuring the world-famous Blue Bar and 'fashion teas'
Wilton Place, Knightsbridge
London SW1X 7RL
UK
T +44 20 7235 6000
E info@the-berkeley.co.uk
W www.the-berkeley.co.uk

Cavalieri Hilton [62]
A luxurious hotel in a hilltop setting
Via Alberto Cadlolo, 101
00136 Rome, Italy
T +39 6 3509 2031
E reservations.rome@hiltonint.com
W www.cavalieri-hilton.it

The Four Seasons [62]
At this luxury hotel, a concierge for teens takes care of all their needs
57 East 57th Street
New York, New York 10022
USA
T +1 212 758 5700
W www.fourseasons.com/newyorkfs

Hôtel de Crillon [63]
The only family-owned palace hotel in Paris
10, place de la Concorde
75008 Paris, France
T +33 1 44 71 15 00
E crillon@crillon.com
W www.crillon.com

Hotel Cipriani [42]
A true testament to the romantic spirit of Venice
Giudecca, 10
30133 Venice, Italy
T +39 41 520 7744
E info@hotelcipriani.it
W www.hotelcipriani.com

Hotel Koffieboontje [67]
Close to the market square, excellent value
Hallenstraat 4
8000 Bruges, Belgium
T +32 50 33 80 27
E info@hotel-koffieboontje.be
W www.hotel-koffieboontje.be

Hotel Monasterio Rocamador [96–97]
This converted 16th-century monastery is now a comfortable hotel
Ctra. Nacional Badajoz – Huelva Km.
41,100 Almendral (Badajoz), Spain
T +34 924 489 000
E mail@rocamador.com
W www.rocamador.com

Hotel Yasmina Merzouga [159]

A beautiful oasis set in the Moroccan sand dunes

Ras Erg Chebbi

Merzouga, Morocco

T +212 61 351 667

E contact@hotelyasminamerzouga.com

W www.hotelyasminamerzouga.com

Mandarin Oriental Hong Kong [63]

The last word in glamour, with breathtaking views over Victoria Harbour

5 Connaught Road

Hong Kong

T +852 2820 4202

E mohkg-reservations@mohg.com

W www.mandarinoriental.com

The Plaza Hotel [54]

Iconic hotel, recently renovated to combine contemporary flair with old-fashioned service

Fifth Avenue at Central Park South

New York, New York 10019

USA

T +1 212 759 3000

E theplaza@fairmont.com

W www.fairmont.com/thePlaza

Renaissance St Pancras Hotel [50]

The revamp of this architectural masterpiece will offer superb rail links at its door

Pancras Road

London NW1 2QP

UK

W www.marriott.com

The View Hotel & Spa [21]

Get close to the sights at the only hotel located inside Monument Valley

Monument Valley Navajo Tribal Park

(four miles east of Highway 163)

Monument Valley, Utah 84536

USA

T +1 435 727 3470

E viewhotelandspa@yahoo.com

W www.monumentvalleyview.com

LODGES, CAMPS

The Desert Homestead and Horsetrails [148, 149]

A stunning spot from which to ride on horseback into the desert

P.O. Box 97448

Maerua Park, Namibia 9000

T +264 61 246 788

E homestead@africaonline.com.na

W www.deserthomestead-namibia.com

Frans Indongo Lodge [26–27]

The perfect stopover between Windhoek and Etosha, but you won't want to leave

P.O. Box 1093

Otjiwarongo, Namibia

T +264 67 687 012

E info@indongolodge.com

W www.indongolodge.com

Mowani Mountain Camp [2–3, 101, 103, 138–142, 149–151]

Just twelve secluded luxury tents with glorious views of the Damara landscape

Onguma Safari Camp [32–35, 102, 144–147]

Watch the local wildlife from the safety and comfort of the hotel veranda and bar

P.O. Box 6784

Windhoek, Namibia

T +264 61 232 009

E mowani@visionsofafrica.com.na

E onguma@visionsofafrica.com.na

W www.mowani.com

Stirling Ridge Log Cabin Resort [16]
Cosy cabins with every necessary amenity
155 Sterling Ridge Drive
Jeffersonville, Vermont 05464
USA
T +1 802 644 8265
E vtcabins@verizon.net
W www.vermont-cabins.com

Wolwedans [158]
*Luxury without pretension, and stunning views
overlooking the sand dunes*
P.O. Box 5048
Windhoek, Namibia
T +264 61 230 616
E info@wolwedans.com.na
W www.wolwedans-namibia.com

CASTLES

Amberley Castle [210]
*Step back in time at this historic castle on
England's South Downs*
Amberley, near Arundel
West Sussex BN18 9LT
UK
T +44 1798 831 992
E info@amberleycastle.co.uk
W www.amberleycastle.co.uk

Château Rigaud [211]
*The service of a hotel with the freedom of
a house party*
33350 Mouliets et Villemartin, France
T +33 5 57 40 78 59
E info@chateaurigaud.co.uk
W www.chateaurigaud.co.uk

Dromoland Castle [1, 206–210]
*A relaxed hotel experience without any
unnecessary fuss and ceremony*
Newmarket-on-Fergus
Co. Clare, Ireland
T +353 61 368 144
E sales@dromoland.ie
W www.dromoland.ie

Taj Lake Palace [211]
*Reminiscent of the Taj Mahal, with a spa for
you and daily entertainment for the children*
Lake Pichola
Udaipur 313001
Rajasthan, India
T +91 294 242 8800
E lakepalace.udaipur@tajhotels.com
W www.tajhotels.com

Torre Palazzone [211]
*This thousand-year-old palazzo provides
21st-century comfort*
Torre Palazzone Sovicille
Siena, Italy
T +39 577 314 364
E info@torrepalazzone.com
W www.torrepalazzone.com

SPAS

Amansala [188]
*An eco-chic resort featuring the world-famous
Bikini Boot Camp*
Tulum, Mexico
T +52 998 185 7428
W www.amansala.com

Epacha Game Lodge & Spa [188]
Safari and pampering: the perfect combination
P.O. Box 362
Outjo, Namibia
T +264 67 697 047
E reservations@epacha.com
W www.epacha.be

The Grove [189]
*Award-winning spa, kids' club and golf course,
and close to London – something for everyone*
Chandler's Cross
Hertfordshire WD3 4TG
UK
T +44 1923 807 807
E info@thegrove.co.uk
W www.thegrove.co.uk

Parrot Cay [189]
*Only an hour from Miami, this private island
features wetlands and a mile-long beach*
Parrot Cay
Turks & Caicos Islands
T +1 649 946 7788
E res@parrotcay.como.bz
W www.parrotcay.como.bz

Taj Exotica Resort & Spa [176–179,
184–185, 189]
*Refined luxury complemented by ayurvedic
treatments and daily yoga sessions*
Wolmar, Flic en Flac
Mauritius
T +230 403 1500
E exotica.mauritius@tajhotels.com
W www.tajhotels.com

KIDS' CLUBS

Évian Royal Resort [194]
Whatever your child's interest, this resort in the French alps has it covered
74501 Évian-Les-Bains, France
T +33 4 50 26 85 00
W www.en.evianroyalresort.com

Frégate Island [195]
Learning about caring for the planet through games in a relaxed environment
Frégate, Seychelles
E reservations@fregate.com
W www.fregate.com

The Ickworth Hotel [194]
This hotel's lovely family atmosphere is enhanced by the spectacular setting
Horringer, Bury St Edmunds
Suffolk IP29 5QE
UK
T +44 1284 735 350
E info@ickworthhotel.co.uk
W www.ickworthhotel.co.uk

Le Saint Géran [133–135, 180–181, 190–191, 195–197]
A wide range of water sports and staff that make each child feel special
Pointe de Flacq
Mauritius
T +230 401 1888
E reservations@
  oneandonlylesaintgeran.com
W www.oneandonlyresorts.com

Sea Island Resort [195]
An institution since 1928, defined by Southern graciousness and hospitality
100 First Street
Sea Island, Georgia 31561
USA
T +1 888 732 4752
E info@seaisland.com
W www.seaisland.com

NATIONAL PARKS

Etosha National Park [102, 103, 188]
114 species of mammals, 340 birds, 110 reptiles, 16 amphibians – one species of fish!
Entrances near Okaukuejo (Andersson Gate) and Namutoni (Von Lindequist Gate), Namibia
W www.namibian.org/travel/
  namibia/etosha.htm

Grand Canyon National Park [17, 21]
A powerful and inspiring landscape that has been in continuous use for over 12,000 years
Grand Canyon, Arizona 86023
USA
T +1 928 638 7888
W www.nps.gov/grca

Monument Valley [20]
This landscape has provided the most enduring and definitive image of the American West
Navajo Tribal Park
Monument Valley, Utah 84536
USA
T +1 435 727 5874
W www.navajonationparks.org

Namib-Naukluft Park [158]
The largest game reserve in Africa, and the fourth-largest in the world
Elena Travel Services & Car Hire CC
P.O. Box 3127
Windhoek, Namibia
E info@namibweb.com
W www.namibweb.com/naukluft.htm

PLACES TO VISIT

Antwerp Zoo [51]
The oldest zoological park in Belgium, located next door to the city's main railway station
Koningin Astridplein 26
2018 Antwerp, Belgium
W www.zooantwerpen.be

Bunratty Castle & Folk Park [212–215]
This 15th-century castle and 19th-century folk park form Ireland's premier visitor attraction
Bunratty
Co. Clare, Ireland
W www.shannonheritage.com

Copenhagen Harbour [55]
Home of the Little Mermaid, the symbol of Denmark and a must-visit
Copenhagen, Denmark
E contact@visitdenmark.com
W www.visitdenmark.com

The Empire State Building [47, 50]
This iconic Art Déco skyscraper stretches more than a quarter of a mile into the sky
350 Fifth Avenue (at 34th Street)

New York, New York 10118
USA
W www.esbnyc.com

The Eiffel Tower [52]
Loved by Parisians and visitors the world over
Champs de Mars
75007 Paris, France
T +33 1 44 11 23 23
W www.tour-eiffel.fr

Greyfriars Bobby [55]
This symbol of companionship and fidelity has
been immortalized in bronze
Candlemaker Row and George IV Bridge
Edinburgh, Scotland
UK
www.greyfriarsbobby.co.uk

Khajuraho Temples [45]
These 10th- and 11th-century temples covered
with erotic carvings are a World Heritage site
Madhya Pradesh, India
W www.khajuraho.org.uk

The London Eye [53]
Spectacular views of landmarks such as the
Houses of Parliament and Westminster Abbey
Riverside Building, County Hall
Westminster Bridge Road
London SE1 7PB
UK
T +44 8709 908 883
E customer.services@londoneye.com
W www.londoneye.com

Somerset House [58–59]
A neoclassical palace on the Thames
Strand
London WC2R 1LA
UK
T +44 20 7845 4600
E info@somersethouse.org.uk
W www.somersethouse.org.uk

The Statue of Liberty [47]
Welcoming visitors and immigrants to
the US since 1886
National Park Service
Statue of Liberty National Monument
Liberty Island
New York, New York 10004
USA
T +1 212 363 3200
W www.nps.gov/stli

TRAIN JOURNEYS

The Arctic Express [17]
An exciting and magical way to search for
Santa Claus
Canterbury Travel (London) Ltd
42 High Street
Northwood, Middlesex HA6 1BL
UK
T +44 1923 822 388
E info@arctic-express.co.uk
W www.arctic-express.co.uk

The Glacier Express [17]
Leisurely train travel in the Swiss Alps
Nordstraße 20
CH-3900 Brig, Switzerland

T +41 27 927 7777
E info@glacierexpress.ch
W www.glacierexpress.ch

Pullman Railtours [17]
Take a ride on historic rail carriages through
New Hampshire's White Mountains
Lincoln, New Hampshire
USA
T +1 603 745 2669
E info@pullmanrailtours.com
W www.pullmanrailtours.com

TRAIN STATIONS

Antwerpen-Centraal [51]
Belgium's finest example of railway architecture
Koningin Astridplein
2000 Antwerp, Belgium
W www.b-rail.be

Grand Central Station [50]
This historic terminus also houses a multitude
of restaurants, cafés and speciality shops
87 East 42nd Street
New York, New York 10017
USA
W http://grandcentralterminal.com

King's Cross Station [50, 54, 55]
The home of Platform 9¾, where Harry and his
friends depart for Hogwarts
Pancras Road
London N1 9AP
UK
T +44 20 7922 4931
W www.networkrail.co.uk

Paddington Station [55]
*Where the beloved character of children's
fiction was discovered by the Brown family*
Praed Street
London W2 1HQ
UK
T +44 20 7922 6793
W www.networkrail.co.uk

St Pancras International Station [50]
*This historic station has been revamped and
features the world's longest Champagne bar*
Pancras Road
London NW1 2QP
UK
T +44 20 7843 4250
W www.stpancras.com

SHIPS, FERRIES

Bateaux-Mouches [67]
*These famous glass-topped boats are a
wonderful introduction to Paris*
Port de la Conférence, Pont de l'Alma
75008 Paris, France
T +33 1 42 25 96 10
E nfo@bateaux-mouches.fr
W www.bateaux-mouches.fr

Caledonian Macbrayne [17]
Island hop in style along Scotland's west coast
Ferry Terminal
Gourock, Scotland PA19 1QP
UK
T +44 8000 665 000
E reservations@calmac.co.uk
W www.calmac.co.uk

Mississippi Queen [17]
*Sail down the great Mississippi River aboard
an historic paddle-wheel steamer*
Mississippi River Cruises
5851 San Felipe, Suite 500
Houston, Texas 77057
USA
T +1 832 252 2494
E contactriver@vacationstogo.com
W www.mississippiqueenriverboat.com

Queen Victoria [17]
*Cunard's latest cruise ship made its maiden
voyage in December 2007*
Richmond House, Terminus Terrace
Southampton SO14 3PN
UK
T +44 845 678 0013
W http://queenvictoria.cunard.co.uk

Star Ferry (Hong Kong) [48–49]
*This picturesque ferry service carries
passengers across Victoria Harbour*
T +852 2367 7065
E sf@starferry.com.hk
W www.starferry.com.hk

SKYRAIL

Skyrail Rainforest Cableway [17]
*Enjoy panoramic views over mountains,
rainforests and waterfalls from the air*
Cairns, Queensland
Australia
E bookings@cairnsattractions.com
W www.cairnsattractions.com

HOLY PLACES

Golden Temple [96]
The most important shrine in the Sikh religion
Amritsar
Punjab, India
W www.amritsar.com

Hagia Sophia [40, 41, 45]
One of history's truly great buildings
Aya Sofya Square, Sultanahmet
Istanbul, Turkey
T +90 212 522 1750

St Peter's Basilica [62]
*Topped by Michelangelo's dome, the basilica is
the traditional resting place of St Peter*
St Peter's Square, Vatican City
Rome, Italy
T +39 6 6988 3712
E stpetersbasilica@gmail.com
W www.saintpetersbasilica.org

Tin Hau Temple [48–49]
Also a popular location for gangster movies!
10 Tin Hau Temple Road
Causeway Bay, Hong Kong
W www.lcsd.gov.hk

MUSEUMS

The Courtauld Gallery [58–59]
*A renowned art collection with a focus on the
Impressionists and Postimpressionists*
Somerset House
Strand
London WC2R 0RN

UK
T +44 20 7848 2526
W www.courtauld.ac.uk/gallery

Designcenter de Winkelhaak [51]
This design centre promoting Belgian
craftsmanship is located near the station
Lange Winkelhaakstraat 26
2060 Antwerp, Belgium
T +32 3 727 1030
E info@winkelhaak.be
W www.winkelhaak.be

Diamantmuseum [51]
The largest museum in the world devoted
entirely to diamonds
Koningin Astridplein 19–23
2018 Antwerp, Belgium
T +32 3 202 4890
E info@diamant.provant.be
W www.diamantmuseum.be

Folklore Museum [67]
Eight 17th-century almshouses form this
window onto Bruges' historic past
Balstraat 43
8000 Bruges, Belgium

Guggenheim Museum [56]
As much about visiting the building as about
the modern art inside
1071 Fifth Avenue (at 89th Street)
New York, New York 10028
USA
T +1 212 423 3500
E visitorinfo@guggenheim.org
W www.guggenheim.org

Hong Kong Maritime Museum [63]
A fascinating look at thousands of years of
Hong Kong's seafaring history
Murray House, Stanley Plaza
Stanley, Hong Kong
T +852 2813 2322
E info@hkmaritimemuseum.org
W www.hkmaritimemuseum.org

Metropolitan Museum of Art [62]
Manhattan's must-visit temple to art
1000 Fifth Avenue
New York, New York 10028
USA
T +1 212 535 7710
W www.metmuseum.org

Musée du Louvre [63]
Catch Mona Lisa's smile here, at one of the
largest, most prestigious museums in the world
Rue de Rivoli
75001 Paris, France
W www.louvre.fr

Museum of Modern Art [51]
Regularly cited as the most influential modern
art museum ever
11 West 53rd Street
New York, New York 10019
USA
T +1 212 708 9400
E info@moma.org
W www.moma.org
Destination Modern Art
W www.moma.org/destination
Red Studio
W http://redstudio.moma.org

South Street Seaport [62]
An historic maritime area with museum, shops
and cafés, and views across the East River
Fulton and South Streets, Pier 17
New York, New York 10038
USA
T +1 212 732 7678
W www.southstreetseaport.com

PARKS, GARDENS

Boston Public Garden [55]
Where charming statues of the ducklings from
a favourite storybook can be found
bordered by Boylston, Arlington, Beacon
and Charles Streets
Boston, Massachusetts
USA
T +1 617 635 4505
E parks@cityofboston.gov
W www.cityofboston.gov/parks

Centennial Park [75]
This large park just southeast of Sydney
features activities and a moonlight cinema
Paddington, Sydney 2021
Australia
T +61 2 9339 6699
E info@cp.nsw.gov.au
W http://centennialparklands.com.au

Central Park [55, 74–75]
Perhaps the most famous park in the world and
home to an ice rink and the Met
bordered by 5th Avenue and Central Park
West, West 59th and West 110th Streets

New York, New York
USA
T +1 212 310 6600
E contact@centralparknyc.org
W www.centralparknyc.org

**Christopher Columbus
Waterfront Park** [75]
*Recently renovated, Boston's first waterside
park is a good place to enjoy the harbour*
Atlantic Avenue
Boston, Massachusetts
USA
T +1 617 635 4505
E parks@cityofboston.gov
W www.cityofboston.gov/parks

Golden Gate Park [75]
*Even bigger than Central Park and home to the
Conservatory of Flowers*
bordered by the Great Highway, Lincoln
Way, Stanyan and Fulton Streets
San Francisco, California
USA
W www.parks.sfgov.org
Japanese Tea Garden
T +1 415 752 1171

Grant Park [55]
*Located in Northeast Portland, near Klickitat
Street, the home of Henry Huggins*
bordered by NE 33rd and NE 36th
Avenues
Portland, Oregon
USA
T +1 503 823 7529
W www.portlandonline.com/parks

Hampstead Heath [75]
*Where such well-known sights as Kenwood
House and Parliament Hill can be found*
Hampstead, London
UK
E hampstead.heath@cityoflondon.gov.uk
W www.cityoflondon.gov.uk

Kensington Gardens [55]
*Adjacent to Hyde Park, this large park contains
Kensington Palace and Peter Pan's statue*
Kensington, London
UK
E hq@royalparks.gsi.gov.uk
W www.royalparks.org.uk

Kungsträdgården [75]
*This 'king's garden' is located in the heart of
the city*
Stockholm, Sweden
E kungstradgarden@chamber.se
W www.kungstradgarden.nu

Manorowen Walled Garden [108]
*An 18th-century kitchen garden with views
across Fishguard Bay*
Goodwick, Fishguard
Pembrokeshire, Wales SA6 5PU
UK
T +44 1348 872 168
W www.onebiggarden.com

Phoenix Park [75]
*This 'largest enclosed urban park in Europe' is
home to deer and livestock*
Dublin, Ireland
T +353 1 677 0095

Richmond Park [75]
*An historic park near the Jacobean stately
home of Ham House*
Richmond, Surrey
UK
E hq@royalparks.gsi.gov.uk
W www.royalparks.org.uk

CAFÉS, BAKERIES,
RESTAURANTS AND BARS

Les Ambassadeurs [63]
*Under the guidance of chef Jean-François
Piège, this acclaimed eatery has two stars*
Hôtel de Crillon
10, place de la Concorde
75008 Paris, France
T +33 1 44 71 16 16
E ambassadeurs@crillon.com
W www.crillon.com

Dining at The Berkeley [63]
*Stylish dining options in London's swanky
Knightsbridge – stop by for a drink or a meal*
Blue Bar
*A stylish bar designed by David Collins in his
distinctive 'Lutyens blue'*
Boxwood Café
*Gordon Ramsay's eatery is an oasis of elegant
chic in the heart of Knightsbridge*
The Berkeley
Wilton Place, Knightsbridge
London SW1X 7RL
UK
T +44 20 7201 1680 (Blue Bar)
T +44 20 7235 1010 (Boxwood Café)
E info@the-berkeley.co.uk

W www.the-berkeley.co.uk
E boxwoodcafe@gordonramsay.com
W www.gordonramsay.com/boxwoodcafe

Le Café Marly [63]
*Enjoying a drink on the terrace overlooking the
Louvre is a true Parisian experience*
Palais du Louvre
93, rue de Rivoli
75001 Paris, France
T +33 1 49 26 06 60

Dining at Cavalieri Hilton [62]
Sup in style in the Eternal City
The Lobby Bar
*Afternoon tea, cocktails and canapés to a
background of piano music*
La Pergola
*Panoramic views over Rome and Michelin-
starred cuisine*
Terrazza del Giardino dell'Uliveto
*A glamorous dining destination overlooking the
hotel pool, featuring classic Italian fare*
Cavalieri Hilton
Via Alberto Cadlolo, 101
00136 Rome, Italy
T +39 6 3509 2152
E lapergolareservations.rome@hilton.com
W www.cavalieri-hilton.it

Dining at The Four Seasons [62]
*A dining experience for every kind of traveller,
from hotel guests to hungry daytrippers*
L'Atelier de Joël Robuchon
Michelin-starred cuisine
The Bar
The place to go for Martinis in Manhattan

TY
Perfect for both afternoon tea and cocktails
The Four Seasons
57 East 57th Street
New York, New York 10022
USA
W www.fourseasons.com/newyorkfs

Harry's Bar [42]
Can there be a better place to drink Bellinis?
Hotel Cipriani
San Marco, 1323
30124 Venezia, Italy
T +39 41 528 5777
E harrysbar@cipriani.com
W www.cipriani.com

Harry's Dolci [42]
*Linger over an espresso and a piece of
zabaglione at this charming waterside café*
Giudecca, 773
30133 Venice, Italy
T +39 41 522 4844
E harrysdolci@cipriani.com
W www.cipriani.com

The Hummingbird Bakery [79]
*Divine bakery tucked away in the hubbub of
Portobello Road Market*
133 Portobello Road, Notting Hill
London W11 2DY
UK
T +44 20 7229 6446
E portobello@hummingbirdbakery.com
W www.hummingbirdbakery.com

Ivar's [84]
*A bowl of clam chowder while watching the
ferry boats arrive is a real Seattle experience*
1001 Alaskan Way, Pier 54
Seattle, Washington 98104
USA
T +1 206 587 6500
W www.ivars.net

Dining at Mandarin Oriental [63]
Tastes of England and France in the Far East
The Chinnery
*Enjoy British dishes and rare single malt
whiskies in a gentleman's club setting*
Pierre
Classic French cuisine in Hong Kong
Mandarin Oriental
5 Connaught Road
Hong Kong
T +852 2522 0111
E mohkg-reservations@mohg.com
W www.mandarinoriental.com

Nannini [79]
*Delicious gelato and more from a beloved
traditional patisserie*
Via Banchi di Sopra
53100 Siena, Italy
T +39 577 236 009
E nannini2@pasticcerienannini.it
W www.pasticcerienannini.it

Restaurant Praq [76]
*Car-shaped tables and a bright colour scheme
are all part of the fun at Praq*
Amstelzijde 37
1184 TX Ouderkerk aan de Amstel

The Netherlands
T +31 20 496 1570
E info@praq.nl
W www.praq.nl

Rick Stein's Restaurants [220]
*This famous chef's four Padstow restaurants
are destinations in their own right*
Rick Stein's Café
*A casual café to drop into for a quick
cappuccino or a three-course dinner*
Middle Street, Padstow
Cornwall PL28 8BQ
UK
St Petroc's Bistro
*Hearty fare to be savoured in view of the
modern art collection or outside in the garden*
New Street, Padstow
Cornwall PL28 8BY
UK
The Seafood Restaurant
*A seafood restaurant located directly opposite
the quay where the fishing boats come in*
Riverside, Padstow
Cornwall PL28 8BY
UK
Stein's Fish & Chips
*A Padstow favourite – choose your fish and
watch it cook while you wait!*
South Quay, Padstow
Cornwall PL28 8BY
UK
T +44 1841 532 700
E reservations@rickstein.com
W www.rickstein.com

S&M Café [80]
*Traditional British comfort food is always
welcome after a long day at the market*
268 Portobello Road
London W10 5TY
UK
T +44 20 8968 8898
E portobello@sandmcafe.co.uk
W www.sandmcafe.co.uk

Starbuck's [84]
*The first Starbuck's store – located in a city
that takes its coffee very seriously*
1912 Pike Place
Seattle, Washington 98101
USA
T +1 206 448 8762
W www.starbucks.com

The Sea Shell Restaurant [79]
*Enjoy fish-and-chips in close proximity to such
attractions as Regents Park zoo*
49–51 Lisson Grove
London NW1 6UH
UK
T +44 20 7224 9000
E enquiry@seashellrestaurant.co.uk
W www.seashellrestaurant.co.uk

Spoon des Îles [195]
*Sister restaurant to chef Alain Ducasse's
acclaimed Spoon Food & Wine in Paris*
Le Saint Géran
Pointe de Flacq, Mauritius
T +230 401 1551
W www.oneandonlyresorts.com

FOOD MARKETS

La Boqueria [84]
*This enormous and hugely popular food market
dates back to the 13th century*
Plaça de la Boqueria
08001 Barcelona, Spain
T +93 318 25 84
E administracio@boqueria.info
W www.boqueria.info

Borough Market [84]
*This London market in the shadow of
Southwark Cathedral is famous the world over*
Southwark Street
London SE1 1TL
UK
T +44 20 7407 1002
E info@boroughmarket.org.uk
W www.boroughmarket.org.uk

Pike Place Market [84]
*Local crafts and a glorious food market make
this a great place to take in the Seattle vibe*
Pike Street
Seattle, Washington 98101
USA
T +1 206 682 7453
E info@pikeplacemarket.org
W www.pikeplacemarket.org

Union Square Greenmarket [84]
*This year-round farmers' market is where
Manhattanites get their fruit and veg*
East 17th Street and Broadway
New York, New York 10003
USA

T +1 212 788 7476
W www.cenyc.org/greenmarket

STREET MARKETS

Bloemenmarkt [84]
Founded in 1862, this is the world's only floating flower market
Singel, between Koningsplein and Muntplein
1017 AX Amsterdam
The Netherlands

Chicago Antique Market [84]
Housed in a beautiful Beaux Arts building, this market is both child- and pet-friendly
Plumbers Hall, West Randolph Street
Chicago, Illinois 60610
USA
T +1 312 666 1200
E info@chicagoantiquemarket.com
W www.chicagoantiquemarket.com

Christkindelsmärik [84]
Everything you could possibly require for your Christmas celebrations
place Broglie and rue de la Comédie
Strasbourg, France
W www.noel-strasbourg.com

Grand Bazaar [84]
Get over jet-lag with a spot of midnight shopping at this 15th-century bazaar
Sultanahmet
Istanbul, Turkey
W www.kapalicarsi.org.tr

Marché aux Puces [84]
The world's first flea market is the place for finding antiques and furniture in Paris
St-Ouen
93400 Paris, France
E info@les-puces.com
W www.les-puces.com

Otavalo Market [84]
A traditional craft market set high in the Andes mountains
Otavlo, Ecuador
E mercadootavalo@yahoo.com
W www.mercadootavalo.com

Portland Saturday Market [84]
This market in Old Town features a Festival of the Last Minute in the run-up to Christmas Eve
between SW Naito Parkway and SW 1st Avenue, under the Burnside Bridge
Portland, Oregon
USA
E info@saturdaymarket.org
W www.portlandsaturdaymarket.com

Portobello Road Market [14, 84]
London at its funky best in this antiques market of long standing
Portobello Road
London W11
UK
E info@portobelloroad.co.uk
W www.portobelloroad.co.uk

SHOPPING

Barney's [62]
A truly elegant shopping experience
660 Madison Avenue
New York, New York 10021
USA
T +1 212 826 8900
E info-madison@barneys.com
W www.barneys.com

Bergdorf Goodman [62]
Follow an afternoon of shopping at Bergdorf's with tea at the Plaza like a true New Yorker
754 Fifth Avenue
New York, New York 10019
USA
T +1 800 558 1855
W www.bergdorfgoodman.com

Caramel [15, 18, 19]
Chic clothing and accessories off London's Westbourne Grove
77 Ledbury Road
London W11 2AG
UK
T +44 20 7727 0906
E info@caramel-shop.co.uk
W www.caramel-shop.co.uk

Honey Jam [80]
Founded by former model Jasmine Guinness, this store features classic toys and cute clothes
267 Portobello Road
London W11 1LR
UK
T +44 20 7243 0449

The Red Teapot Arcade [83]

*An arcade along busy Portobello Road
crammed with antiques stalls*
101–103 Portobello Road
London W11 2QB
UK
T +44 20 7727 5240

FESTIVALS

Holi [88–89]

*Hindu festival in early spring, also known as the
Festival of Colours*
India
E festivalsindex@yahoo.com
W www.holifestival.org

Cinco de Mayo [94]

*Popular with schoolchildren in the US, this
Mexican holiday features candy-stuffed piñatas*
Mexico, but primarily USA
W www.cincodemayo.org

Notting Hill Carnival [95]

*A riotous celebration in West London that
honours the area's Caribbean heritage*
Notting Hill, London W11
UK
W www.nottinghillcarnival.biz

Puerto Rican Day Parade [94]

*Held on the second Sunday in June, this parade
is a Manhattan tradition and an all-day event*
New York, New York
USA
W www.nationalpuertoricandayparade.org

FARMS, RANCHES

The Inn at Celebrity Dairy [115]

*Stay year-round at this 300-acre working dairy
in rural Chatham County*
144 Celebrity Dairy Way
Siler City, North Carolina 27344
USA
T +1 919 742 5176
E theinn@celebritydairy.com
W www.celebritydairy.com

Inn Serendipity [115]

*This bed-and-breakfast has been recognized as
one of the top eco-destinations in the US*
7843 County P
Browntown, Wisconsin 53522
USA
T +1 608 329 7056
E info@innserendipity.com
W www.innserendipity.com

Lavender Hill Farm [115]

*Explore nearby historic Lexington while enjoying
a relaxing stay at this friendly farm*
1374 Big Spring Drive
Lexington, Virginia 24450
USA
T +1 540 464 5877
E info@lavhill.com
W www.lavhill.com

Liberty Hill Farm [115]

*Stay at this 1825 farmhouse in the heart of
New England, family-run since 1979*
511 Liberty Hill Road
Rochester, Vermont 05767

USA
T +1 802 767 3926
E beth@libertyhillfarm.com
W www.libertyhillfarm.com

Mary Jane's Farm [115]

*Mary Jane offers a bed-and-breakfast,
workshops, farm produce – and a magazine!*
1000 Wild Iris Lane
Moscow, Idaho 83843
USA
T +1 888 750 6004
E iris@maryjanesfarm.org
W www.maryjanesfarm.org

North Country Farms [115]

*Organic produce and a location near Hanalei
Bay are just part of this island farm's appeal*
P.O. Box 723, Kilauea
Kauai, Hawaii 96754
USA
T +1 808 828 1513
E ncfarms@aloha.net
W www.northcountryfarms.com

The Philo Apple Farm [115]

*An organic farm in California offering guest
cottages and cooking classes*
18501 Greenwood Road
Philo, California 95466
USA
T +1 707 895 2333
E karen@philoapplefarm.com
W www.philoapplefarm.com

Valley Dream Farm [114–115]

*An organic farm with a conscience, donating
produce to community organizations*

5901 Pleasant Valley Road
Cambridge, Vermont 05444
USA
T +1 802 644 6598
W www.localharvest.org/farms

ROAD TRIPS

The Germany Fairy-Tale Road [120]

*A 600-kilometre road from Hanau to Bremen
follows the trail of the Brothers Grimm*

Deutsche Märchenstraße
Kurfürstenstraße, 9
34117 Kassel, Germany
T +49 561 9204 7910
E info@deutsche-maerchenstrasse.de
W www.deutsche-maerchenstrasse.com

WATERSPORTS

Surf School Lanzarote [127]

*Students can also stay at this surf school in the
beautiful Canary Islands*

Playa de Famara
Lanzarote, Canary Islands
E info@surfschoollanzarote.com
W www.surfschoollanzarote.com

SAND DUNES

Great Sand Dunes National Park [159]

*Activities on offer include horseback riding,
bison tours and 'sandboarding''*

11999 Highway 150 (visitor centre)
Mosca, Colorado 81146
USA
T +1 719 378 6300
W www.nps.gov/grsa

Red and White Sand Dunes [159]

Spectacular sand dunes in a tropical setting

Muí Ne Beach, Phan Thiet
Bính Thuan, Vietnam
W www.muinebeach.net

Sam Sand Dunes [159]

*Include a visit to the dunes with a trip to the
Golden Fort, Jaisalmer's premier attraction*

Jaisalmer
Rajasthan, India
W www.indiasite.com/rajasthan/
     jaisalmer/samsanddunes.html

Sossusvlei Sand Dunes [103, 158–163]

*The best time to visit the dunes is just after
dawn, to escape the heat of the noonday sun*

Namib-Naukluft Park
Namibia
E info@namibian.org
W www.namibian.org

Te Paki Sand Dunes [159]

*The golden dunes of Te Paki are a popular
destination in New Zealand*

Far North Road (field centre)
Te Paki, Cape Reinga 0480
New Zealand
T +64 9 409 8101
W www.doc.govt.nz

**White Sands
National Monument** [159]

*The White Sands park participates in the
Junior Ranger scheme, for 5- to 12-year-olds*

Highway 70, 24 kilometres southwest
of Alamogordo (visitor centre)
New Mexico
USA
T +1 505 679 2599
W www.nps.gov/whsa

THEME PARKS

Aqualand [216, 217]

*A water amusement park located near Spain's
Guadalete River*

Old road N-IV from El Puerto de Santa
María to Jerez, exit 646
11500 El Puerto de Santa María
Cádiz, Spain
T +34 902 11 49 9
W www.aspro-ocio.es/bahiadecadiz

Harbour Park [216]

*Visit Harbour Park for a fun family day out on
England's South Coast*

Seafront, Littlehampton
West Sussex BN17 5LL
UK
T +44 1903 721 200
W www.harbourpark.com

Hong Kong Disneyland [63]

*This location in the Far East is the fifth, and the
smallest, addition to the Disneyland family*

Penny's Bay

Lantau Island, Hong Kong
T +852 1 830 830
W http://park.hongkongdisneyland.com

Parc Astérix [216]
Easily accessible from Paris, this park features a
wooden roller-coaster called 'Tonnerre de Zeus'
60128 Plailly, France
T +33 826 30 10 40
E contact@parcasterix.com
W www.parcasterix.fr

Rye Playland [216]
This national landmark does not charge
admission and has a carousel dating to 1915
Playland Parkway
Rye, New York 10580
USA
T +1 914 813 7010
W www.ryeplayland.org

Santa Cruz Beach Boardwalk [216]
This beloved park has appeared in such cult
movies as Dirty Harry and The Lost Boys
400 Beach Street
Santa Cruz, California 95060
USA
T +1 831 423 5590
E guest.services@scseaside.com
W www.beachboardwalk.com

Shilp Gram [216]
An arts and crafts centre featuring museums,
performances, and camel rides
Bgore Ki Haveli, Gangaur Ghat
Udaipur
313001 Rajasthan, India

T +91 294 243 1304
E wzcccom_jp1@sancharnet.in
W www.wzccindia.com/shilpgram

Tivoli Gardens [216]
During the summer months, Tivoli also features
a live music series, Fredagsrock (Friday Rock)
3 Vesterbrogade
1630 Copenhagen, Denmark
T +45 3315 1001
W www.tivoli.dk

Wild Wadi [216]
An outdoor park within sight of the splendid
Burj Al-Arab hotel
Jumeirah Beach Road
Dubai, United Arab Emirates
T +971 4 348 4444
E info@wildwadi.com
W www.wildwadi.com

Wurstelprater [216]
After a ride on the Ferris wheel, tuck in to
potato fritters and Stelze (pork knuckle)
Prater 9
1020 Vienna, Austria
T +43 1 728 0516
E info@wiener-prater.at
W www.wiener-prater.at

RENTING PROPERTIES

National Trust Cottages [231]
Eschew hotels and do as the Brits do by opting
for a charming self-catering cottage
Holiday Booking Office
P.O. Box 536

Melksham, Wiltshire SN12 8SX
UK
T +44 844 800 2070
E cottages@nationaltrust.org.uk
W www.nationaltrustcottages.co.uk

National Trust for Scotland
Holidays [231]
When in Scotland and in search of a cottage or
a bothy, NTS will have the solution
Wemyss House
28 Charlotte Square
Edinburgh, Scotland EH2 4ET
UK
T +44 131 243 9331
E holidays@nts.org.uk
W www.ntsholidays.com/cottages

Online resources to aid and inspire, for whatever kind of holiday you are planning

PLAN

Airline Angels
Child care for families on the move
www.airlineangels.co.uk

AudioAble
Download books to listen to on the plane
www.audioable.com

Babies Travel Lite
Diapers, formula, and more delivered to your home or to holiday destinations abroad
www.babiestravellite.com

Baby-Friendly Boltholes
Stylish accommodation that is especially baby-friendly
www.babyfriendlyboltholes.co.uk

Baby Goes 2
Advice and reports on family-friendly destinations and resorts
www.babygoes2.com

Black Tomato
Cool and funky travel company
www.blacktomato.co.uk

Britain's Finest
The UK's best hotels, B&Bs and attractions
www.britainsfinest.co.uk

Cruise Critic
Reviews and useful information for first-time travellers
www.cruisecritic.co.uk

Delicious Baby
Online forum, plus tips on planning and packing for family holidays
www.deliciousbaby.com

Family Safe Plus
Keep travel documents online (and secure), accessible from anywhere
www.familysafeplus.co.uk

Fare Compare
Good tips on fare upgrades for travel in the US
www.farecompare.com

First Choice
UK-based company that will organize any kind of family holiday you can think of
www.firstchoice.co.uk

Flight 001
A design-forward store offering space-saving luggage and compact travel games
www.flight001.com

Google Earth
Get a bird's-eye view of wherever you are, wherever you want to be
www.earth.google.com

Google Maps
Interactive maps with 360° street photography
www.maps.google.co.uk

Greenbee
A group of travel services under one cyber roof
www.greenbee.com

Gusto
US-based site featuring travel advice and recommendations
www.gusto.com

Holiday Taxis
Arrange your airport transfer in advance
www.holidaytaxis.com

Holidays With Kids
Australian-based online guide to family travel
www.holidayswithkids.com.au

I-Escape
For those who want something a little different
www.i-escape.com

Kids Can Travel
Planning holidays around your kids' interests
www.kidscantravel.com

Kids Europe
A great holiday-planning site with kids in mind
www.kidseurope.com

Late Rooms
Get up to 70 per cent off published rates
www.laterooms.com

Le Travel Store
Links and top tens for every possible travel essential, garment and accessory
www.letravelstore.com

Life's 2 Short
Will take care of flights, tickets, villa rental, child care – the lot
www.lifes2short.co.uk

Little Eco
UK-based shop featuring natural products for babies and children, skincare for mummies
www.littleeco.com

Madallie
An online travel store with a focus on children's toys and supplies
www.madallie.com

The Man In Seat 61
Directs you to the best train routes worldwide
www.seat61.com

My Baby Boutique
Online store with great educational toys
www.mybabyboutique.net

Nine Blue
Essential information for creating a family trip
www.nineblue.com

One Bag
'The art and science of travelling light'
www.onebag.com

Pet Travel
Pet-friendly accommodation
www.pettravel.com

Powder Byrne
Holidays from the beach to the slopes
www.powderbyrne.com

Priority Pass
Membership into the world's airport lounges
www.prioritypass.com

Quintessentially
International members' network that takes care of every element of your holiday
www.quintessentially.com

Rick Steves
'Europe through the back door' with American Public Television's favourite tour guide
www.ricksteves.com

Seat Guru
The definitive guide to airline seating
www.seatguru.com

Simply Parking
Takes the hassle out of parking at the airport
www.simplyparking.co.uk

Small Families
Specializing in single-parent holidays
www.smallfamilies.co.uk

Take The Family
Hand-picked holidays and breaks for families
www.takethefamily.com

TeleAdapt
Helping hotels and their guests stay connected
www.teladapt.com

Tiny Tots Away
Delivering all your baby essentials directly to your hotel
www.tinytotsaway.com

Travel For Kids
A listing of fun things to do with children
www.travelforkids.com

Travel Jungle
UK-based fare comparison site
www.traveljungle.co.uk

Travel Post
Travel reviews and other useful information
www.travelpost.com

Travel Supermarket
Refers you to the best sites for competitive prices
www.travelsupermarket.com

Travel Turtle
Provides country-specific vaccination information
www.travelturtle.co.uk

Travel Zoo
Cheap flights, hotels, cruises, car hire, and more
www.travelzoo.com

Traveling Chic
Trendy luggage and travel accessories
www.travelingchic.com

Travelling With Children
Advice and services for travelling with kids
www.travellingwithchildren.co.uk

Trip Advisor
Honest reviews from people who have been there
www.tripadvisor.co.uk

Trip Connect
A place to connect with friends and share travel advice
www.tripconnect.com

TripIt
Offering travel assistance to save you time and energy
www.tripit.com

UNESCO World Heritage Sites
Get inspired for a truly memorable holiday experience
http://whc.unesco.org

The Visa Company
Leading online service for visas and passports
www.thevisacompany.com

World Climate
Find out about rainfall, temperature, and other weather conditions around the globe
www.worldclimate.com

World Reviewer
Reviews by and inspiration from independent travellers
www.worldreviewer.com

Your Safe Planet
Free advice on chosen destinations
www.yoursafeplanet.co.uk

CITY

Art Culture
All that is new and current in art and culture
www.artculture.com

Best Restaurants
Search for restaurants across Australia
www.bestrestaurants.com.au

Boutique India
A personal service for planning family holidays to India
www.boutiqueindia.com

Children's Concierge
Helping children explore the world's great cities with customized activities
www.childrensconcierge.com

City Story Walks
Walking tours and city stories that can be downloaded onto an MP3 player
www.citystorywalks.com

European City Parks
A guide to Europe's parks and gardens
www.european-city-parks.com

Family Friendly
Child-friendly events and museums in the UK
www.familyfriendly.org.uk

Florence Guides
Walking tours for kids, with themes including 'Renaissance Florence' and 'Medieval Florence'
www.florenceguides.com

Go City Kids
City guides for parents
www.gocitykids.parentsconnect.com

Green City Walks
Explore London with a planned walk
www.greencitywalks.com

Kid Friendly Guide
View menus created with kids in mind and choose a restaurant
www.kidfriendlyguide.com

London Markets
Directory of London markets with opening times
www.londonmarkets.co.uk

Museum Stuff
An online directory for museums across the world and across genres
www.museumstuff.com

Museums USA
Find over 15,000 museums across the USA
www.museumsusa.org

Paris Muse
Private tours for families in the great museums of Paris
www.parismuse.com

Queen Victoria Market
A cosmopolitan food market in Melbourne, Australia
www.qvm.com.au

Seven Stories
Museum in Newcastle that celebrates Britain's rich heritage of children's literature
www.sevenstories.org.uk

Show Me
Child-orientated guide to the UK's galleries and museums
www.show.me.uk

Taste Space
New York restaurant guide
www.tastespace.com

Via Michelin
Street maps and route-planning across Europe
www.viamichelin.com

Where Can We Go
A guide to what's on in the UK
www.wherecanwego.com

Zagat
Popular online reference guide to restaurants all over the world
www.zagat.com

ADVENTURE

Arctic Experience
An Icelandic adventure astride native ponies
www.arctic-experience.co.uk

Agritourism In Italy
A guide to all things agritouristic in Italy
www.agritourism.it

Bali Island Horse
Horseback riding in Bali on Yeh Ganga Beach
www.baliislandhorse.com

Bedruthan Hotel
A hotel in Cornwall that will appeal to kids
www.bedruthan.com

Big Blue Air Touring
Adventures in the Australian Outback
www.bigblueairtouring.com

Bigland Hall Equestrian
Horseback riding in England's Lake District
www.biglandhall.com

The Blue Train
Luxurious train travel in South Africa
www.luxurytrains.co.za

Camp Beaumont
Great camping holidays for kids
www.campbeaumont.co.uk

Camping and Caravaning Club
Camping and caravanning sites in the UK
www.campingandcaravanningclub.co.uk

Caper Travel Company
Camel safaris in Rajasthan
www.capertravelindia.com

North American Riding for the Handicapped
A listing of centres in the US offering hippotherapy
www.narha.org

Catalina Island Camps
A Californian summer camp featuring snorkelling, kayaking, more
www.catalinaislandcamps.com

Corbett Hideaway
Birdwatching safaris in India
www.corbetthideaway.com

DoppelReiter-Reisen
Riding holidays in the Camargue
www.doppelreiter-reisen.de

Dune Guide
A comprehensive guide to the world's most impressive sand dunes
www.duneguide.com

Enid Blyton
Buy the books and start the holiday adventure!
www.enidblyton.net

Equine Adventures
International horseriding holidays, organized by continent
www.equineadventures.co.uk

eTravelogue
Tools to plan the perfect road trip
www.etravelogue.com

Families Worldwide
Activity and adventure holidays with tailor-made itineraries
www.familiesworldwide.co.uk

Gordon's Guide
A huge variety of adventure vacations, including horseback riding in Texas
www.gordonsguide.com

Hidden Trails
Equestrian and other outdoor holidays around the world
www.hiddentrails.com

Hip Chalets
Cool chalet accommodation in Chamonix, France
www.hipchalets.com

Holiday Adventure
Outdoor activities and day camps for kids at a prep school in Surrey
www.holiday-adventure.com

Hooked On Nature
Suggested reading material for children interested in the Great Outdoors
www.hookedonnature.org

Horse Fun
Tips, quizzes, more for kids who love horses
www.horsefun.com

Kids In Tow
The adventure-holiday specialist
www.kidsintow.co.uk

Kids Sea Camp
Scuba lessons in the Cayman Islands
www.kidsseacamp.com

MultiMap
Useful information, including directions covering a wide host of countries
www.multimap.com

My Jungfrau
For a Swiss adventure holiday with a difference
www.myjungfrau.ch

Olive Grove
The best place to stay when in Windhoek, Namibia
www.olivegrove-namibia.com

Ordnance Survey
View these renowned maps online
www.ordnancesurvey.co.uk

The Pacific Coast Highway
Head up California's coastline for unbeatable views, stopping at Big Sur and Monterey
www.us-101.com

Picnics On The Piste
A company that will bring the picnic to you!
www.picnicsonthepiste.com

Puffin Express
Small group tours in the Highlands and islands of Scotland
www.puffinexpress.co.uk

Rand McNally
Get driving routes and updates on roads and traffic
www.randmcnally.com

The Resort At Paws Up
A resort in Montana offering a variety of adventure activities
www.pawsup.com

Route 66
The oldest website devoted to the most famous road-trip route in the world
www.historic66.com

Running-R Guest Ranch
Stay on a real Texan dude ranch!
www.rrranch.com

Save Our Snow
Learn how global warming is affecting snowfall, ski resorts and glaciers
www.saveoursnow.com

Scooby Campers
1960s vans for hire in Scotland, complete with sat nav
www.scoobycampers.com

Snail Trail
Classic campers with Cath Kidston-style interiors, to hire when travelling around the UK
www.snailtrail.co.uk

Travel Alberta
Holidays in the Canadian Rockies
www.travelalberta.com

Trekking For Kids
Join a trek in Spain or up Mt Kilimanjaro
www.trekkingforkids.org

The Umalas Equestrian Resort Bali
Take a ride on horseback on the beach in Bali
www.balionhorse.com

Vintage Surfari Wagons
Rent a VW camper van for a 'surfari'!
www.vwsurfari.com

Vroom Vroom Vroom
Car-rental comparison site
www.vroomvroomvroom.co.uk

Whale and Dolphin Conservation Society
Protecting these animals and their environment
www.wdcs.org

Whistler Blackcomb Ski Resort
Ski down the slopes or ride on horseback
www.whistlerblackcomb.com

Whitepod
A five-star winter safari camp in the Swiss Alps
www.whitepod.com

ESCAPE

Abercrombie & Kent
The original luxury travel specialists
www.abercrombiekent.com

After-the-Baby Boot Camp
An addition to the Bikini Boot Camp package, this one is even better for mother and baby
www.afterthebabybootcamp.com

The Amazing Hedge Puzzle
A fun site dedicated to a maze in Herefordshire, with history, puzzles, more
www.mazes.co.uk

Beachcomber
Specialists in luxury travel, with destinations to Mauritius and the Seychelles
www.beachcombertours.co.uk

Cedar Log Homes
Log cabins to rent in the US, organized by state
www.cedar-log-homes.com

The Elms
A welcoming family retreat in Worcestershire with a stand-out kids' club
www.theelmshotel.co.uk

Exclusive Resorts
Resorts on the beach, in the mountains, or in the city
www.exclusiveresorts.com

Expressions Families
Luxury holidays for families
www.expressionsholidays.co.uk

Forte Village
A beachside resort in Sardinia
www.fortevillage.com

Irish Cottage Holidays
Self-catering accommodation from thatched cottages to flats for rent throughout Ireland
www.irishcottageholidays.com

Lajitas
Visit this luxurious resort and spa in Pancho Villa country
www.lajitas.com

Lakelover
Cottages for hire in the 'Heart of the Lakes'
www.lakelover.co.uk

Linthwaite House Hotel
A country-house hotel located deep in the heart of the Lake District
www.linthwaite.com

Mediterranean Experience
Romantic escapes and short breaks around the Mediterranean Sea
www.medexperience.co.uk

Quo Vadis?
Takes care of all your luxury-holiday planning
www.quovadistravel.co.uk

Smoky Mountain Mall
Rent a log cabin in Tennessee's Smoky Mountains
www.smokymtnmall.com

Tots Too
Luxury holidays for families with young children
www.totstoo.com

Villazzo
Boutique hotel group, with locations in Miami, Aspen, St Tropez, Courchevel, Paris and Marbella
www.villazzo.com

My deepest gratitude to all those involved in making this book
an extraordinary adventure. With special thanks to Antonia
Steyn, Claire Fulton, Christina Wilson, Rachna Makwana and
Mary-Anne Scorer, and to Pam McAlpine and Joan Hunter
for the use of their family photographs. Thank you, too, to
Elain McAlpine, my editor, who put in so much more to this
book than her role demanded. And finally to my dear husband
and children, I treasure each moment of our ongoing journey
together – with love always.

Sarah Hogan www.sarahhogan.co.uk 1, 204, 206–209, 212–215, 231 (bottom), 254 (right), 255
(right); Antonia Steyn, assistant Claire Fulton www.oneleague.co.za 2–3, 6, 7, 10, 12–13, 26, 27,
30–34, 35 (Claire Fulton, lower left), 98–99, 101, 102, 172–174, 176, 178–187, 190–193, 196–199,
202, 203, 234–235, 236 (middle), 237, 244–253, 254 (middle), 255 (middle), 256; Christina Wilson
www.christinawilson.co.uk 5, 24, 25 (middle), 36–44, 45 (middle and bottom), 46–49, 50 (top), 51
(top and middle), 52, 53, 58–61, 64 (middle and right), 66–67, 70–71, 75, 76 (middle), 77, 84–86,
90–93, 94 (middle), 95 (bottom), 96, 97, 200–201, 216, 217, 218 (right), 220–222, 228, 229, 230
(middle and bottom), 231 (top), 232, 233, 236 (top and bottom), 238–241, 255 (left); Heather
Lewin www.heatherlewin.com 15, 18, 19, 22, 23, 64 (left), 78–83; David Jackson and Helen Beuschel
www.davidjacksonphotography.co.uk 16, 17, 20, 25 (top and bottom), 50 (bottom), 51 (bottom), 56,
56–57, 68, 69, 74, 76 (left and right), 218 (left), 223, 224, 225, 226, 227, 231 (middle), 242, 243;
Miranda Warbarton 45 (top), 72, 73, 88, 89, 104, 105, 106, 107, 108, 109, 218 (middle), 230 (top),
254 (left); David Garner www.garnerphoto.co.uk 50 (middle), 54, 55; Cavalieri Hilton 62 (top); The
Four Seasons 62 (middle); Mandarin Oriental 63 (top); The Berkeley (64 (middle); Hôtel de
Crillon 62 (bottom), 63 (bottom); Ray Laskowitz/Lonely Planet Images 94 (top); AFP/AFP 94
(bottom); Leon Neal/AFP 95 (top); Stephen Chernin/Getty Images News 95 (middle); Kempinski
Pragelato Village 164–166; Tim Pannell/Corbis 168 (top); Richard Gardette/zefa/Corbis 168
(middle); Nice One Productions/Corbis 168 (bottom); Doug Berry/Corbis 169 (top); Kay
Nietfeld/epa/Corbis 169 (middle); Justin Cash/Brand X/Corbis 169 (bottom); Epacha Game Lodge
& Spa 188 (top); Amansala 188 (middle); Taj Exotica Resort & Spa 188 (bottom), 189 (middle);
The Grove 189 (top); Parrot Cay 189 (bottom); Évian Royal Resort 194 (top); The Ickworth
Hotel 194 (middle); Sea Island Resort 194 (bottom), 195 (top); Le Saint Géran 195 (middle);
Frégate Island 195 (bottom); Dromoland Castle 210 (top); Amberley Castle 210 (middle and
bottom); Château Rigaud 211 (top); Taj Lake Palace 211 (middle); Torre Palazzone 211 (bottom).

Special thanks to Caramel, London, who allowed us to photograph in their beautiful store.

First published in the United Kingdom in 2008
by Thames & Hudson Ltd, 181A High Holborn,
London WC1V 7QX

www.thamesandhudson.com

FamilyLifeStyle: Travel © 2008 Thames & Hudson Ltd,
London
Text © 2008 Anita Kaushal

British Library Cataloguing-in-Publication Data
A catalogue record for this book is available
from the British Library

ISBN 978-0-500-51423-8

Printed and bound in China by
C & C Offset Printing Co Ltd